A NEW OWNER'S
GUIDE TO
YORKSHIRE
TERRIERS

JG-128

Opposite page: Ch. Steppin' Up Billy the Kid owned by Janet Jackson.

The author acknowledges the contribution of Judy Iby of the following chapters: Sport of Purebred Dogs, Identification and Finding the Lost Dog, Traveling with Your Dog, Health Care, Behavior and Canine Communication.

PHOTO CREDITS:

Isabelle Francais: 1, 8, 9, 11, 13, 17, 21, 26, 30, 33, 34, 35, 36, 37, 40, 41, 45, 47, 49, 51, 54, 57, 59, 62, 64, 65, 66, 71, 73, 74, 78, 80, 81, 83, 84, 87, 90, 93, 95, 97, 98, 101, 103, 104, 105, 109, 117, 127, 129, 130, 131, 139, 141, 155

T.F.H. Publications, Inc.
One TFH Plaza
Third and Union Avenues
Neptune City, NJ 07753

This book has been published with the intent to provide accurate and authoritative information in regard to the subject matter within. While every precaution has been taken in preparation of this book, the author and publisher expressly disclaim responsibility for any errors, omissions, or adverse effects arising from the use or application of the information contained herein. The techniques and suggestions are used at the reader's discretion and are not to be considered a substitute for veterinary care. If you suspect a medical problem, consult your veterinarian.

ISBN 0-7938-2777-9

www.tfh.com

A New Owner's Guide to YORKSHIRE TERRIERS

Janet Jackson

Contents

2004 Edition

The Yorkshire Terrier is renowned for his beautiful coat.

6 • Dedication

8 • History of the Yorkshire Terrier
Origins • The Yorkshire in England •
The Yorkshire in the United States

19 • Standard for the Yorkshire Terrier
The Kennel Club Breed Standard • The
American Kennel Club Breed Standard
• Interpretation of the Standards

34 • Characteristics of the Yorkshire Terrier
Hunter • Watchdog • Human Companion

39 • Selecting a Yorkshire Terrier
Finding a Breeder • Deciding to Breed •
Picking a Puppy • Adopting an Older
Dog • The Importance of Spaying and
Neutering

55 • Caring for Your Yorkshire Terrier
Household Dangers • Handling •
Housetraining • Feeding and Nutrition •
Grooming • Grooming for the Show

71 • Dental Care for Your Yorkshire Terrier
Chewing • Visiting the Vet • Periodontal
Disease • Maintaining Oral Health

77 • Health Care for Your Yorkshire Terrier
Physical Exams • Common Canine
Diseases • Intestinal Parasites • Other
Internal Parasites • External Parasites •
Other Medical Problems • Spaying and
Neutering

Chewing is a necessary part of a Yorkie's development.

The Yorkie's distinctive coat needs proper grooming.

147 • **Traveling With Your Dog**
Car Rides • Air Travel • Boarding Kennels

153 • **Identification and Finding the Lost Dog**
Collars and Tags • Tattoos • Microchips • Finding the Lost Dog

98 • **Breeding Your Yorkshire Terrier**
Making the Decision • Preparing to Breed • Pregnancy and Labor • The Birth • After the Birth • Selling the Puppies

107 • **Sport of Purebred Dogs**
Puppy Kindergarten • Canine Good Citizen® Program • Conformation • Obedience • Tracking • Agility • Performance Tests • General Information

Dental health is essential for all Yorkshire Terriers.

129 • **Behavior and Canine Communication**
Socialization and Training • Problem Behaviors

157 • **Resources**

159 • **Index**

Your Yorkie should be socialized with other animals from an early age.

Dedication

This book is dedicated to
Ch. Shadomountin Steppin'Up, "Burt"–
my best buddy, my bodyguard, and the
foundation of all the Steppin'Up Yorkies.

HISTORY of the Yorkshire Terrier

ORIGINS

The Yorkshire Terrier did not begin as the fashionable and glamorous breed that he is today. He is a combination of so-called terrier breeds, evolving in the fields and the homes of serfs, craftsmen, and weavers of Yorkshire, England's largest shire. The serfs in England were not allowed to have hunting dogs; they were only allowed to have small dogs, which were mostly used to kill rats and other varmints. One of these small dogs, the Waterside Terrier, was described as a small, long-coated dog, occasionally grizzly (bluish-grey) in color, weighing anywhere from 6 to 20 pounds, but usually around 10 pounds.

This Waterside Terrier was often crossed with the old English or Manchester Terrier, a silky-coated black-and-tan or blue-and-tan terrier who weighed around 5 pounds and was an exceptional ratter

Although well known as a glamorous and fashionable breed today, the Yorkshire Terrier originally evolved in the homes of serfs, craftsmen, and weavers.

The ancestors of the Yorkshire Terrier were prized for their ability to kill rats and other varmints.

around the homestead. Ratting contests were a pastime often held by the local innkeepers to bring patronage to their pubs. Small size and ratting ability were the most sought-after points in a dog.

THE YORKSHIRE IN ENGLAND

With the beginning of the Industrial Revolution in the late 1700s, crafters from Scotland went south to Yorkshire, England, to find work in the mills as weavers. They brought with them several "Scotch" terriers. Among these terriers was the Paisley Terrier, a small, silky-coated dog of various shades of blue weighing no more than 16 pounds. Another was the Clydesdale Terrier from the Glasgow region on the river Clyde, described as "desired to be a bright steel blue extending from the back of the head to the root of the tail and on no account intermingled with any fawn, light or dark hairs. The head, legs and feet should be a clear bright golden tan free from grey, sooty or dark hairs. The tail should be very dark blue or black. Coat as long and straight as possible, free from all traces of curl or waviness, very glossy, silky in texture." The result of the crossing of these breeds was the Yorkshire Terrier, because the Yorkshire area is where it all took place.

In 1873, the Kennel Club of England was formed to record pedigrees and to provide a code of rules for dog shows and field trials that were emerging. Dogs were divided into two groups: Non-Sporting and Sporting. The Yorkshire Terrier joined the 40 selected Non-Sporting breeds under the name of Broken-Haired Scotch and Yorkshire Terriers.

Huddersfield Ben is considered to be the father of the breed. Born in 1865, the inbred offspring of a mother-son breeding, he possessed the rare ability to pass his virtues to his progeny. He was a great sire, with many of his offspring winning at shows. Ben was bred by Mr. W. Eastwood of Huddersfield. His sire and dam came from Yorkshire specimens tracing back to most of the better-known Yorkshire and Lancashire dogs and bitches of the time. He was acquired by Mr. and Mrs. Jonas Foster of Bradford, who were ardent fanciers and showed him to many wins. Ben died in 1871; he was unquestionably the best specimen seen at that time, and judges recognized his merits, giving him many prizes. This laid down the real foundation for the breed.

THE YORKSHIRE IN THE UNITED STATES

The emergence of the Yorkshire Terrier in the United States began in the late 19th century, and the breed became a popular pet as well as one of the early show dogs.

Dog showing began in the US in the 1870s. The American Kennel Club (AKC) was formed on September 17, 1884, in Philadelphia. The first Yorkshire Terrier to have an American Kennel Club registered number was Butch (5376), owned by Charles Andrews of Bloomington, Illinois. The first Yorkie to appear in the AKC studbook was Belle, owned by Mrs. A.E. Godeffroy. Mr. P.H. Coombs claimed in 1890 that his Bradford Harry was the only Yorkie to have become an American champion. However, Ch. Hero, imported by Mr. and Mrs. Henry Kisteman, was listed in shows as a champion in 1883 and 1884. During the 1870s and 1880s, the Kistemans of New York City were the most successful exhibitors of Yorkies, and Ch. Hero's bloodlines can be traced to the Yorkies of the 1920s.

Mrs. Fred Senn of New York did have a strain that can be traced to the present. She showed her first Yorkie in 1878, and she bred the first American-bred champion, Ch. Queen of the Fairies. Her dog may be followed up to Mrs. Goldie Stone's Ch. Petit Byngo

The Yorkshire Terrier became a popular pet and show dog beginning in the late 19th century.

Boy. Mrs. Stone's Petit Kennel became quite famous, and her dogs still appear in many of today's pedigrees.

In 1898, Mr. L. Cullen imported several dogs, including Ch. Bradford Ben, one of Mrs. Foster's top winners in England. Mrs. Anna Radcliffe, of Gold Mount Yorkshires, owned a bitch called Lady Blue who can be traced back to Huddersfield Ben within five generations. She was the dam of Mrs. Radcliffe's Gold Mount Gay Boy.

During the period from 1900 to 1920, there were 45 Yorkshire Terrier champions recorded. However, at the end of World War I, there were only eight American and two Canadian breeders of Yorkies left.

Mrs. Harold Riddock was one of the breeders who managed to carry on during these hard times. In 1924, she took over Anna Radcliffe's Gold Mount Yorkshires. These dogs formed the foundation for Mrs. Goldie Stone's Petit, Harry Smith's Haslington, and Mr. and Mrs. Arthur Mills' Millbarry Yorkshires.

In 1931, Mrs. Goldie Stone purchased her future champion, Petit Byngo Boy, from Mrs. Riddock. He was a big winner in the 1930s. Her breeding program was really the turning point for the Yorkshire Terrier in America. She combined the older American and Canadian lines to produce many top winners. Her Ch. Petit Magnificent Prince was the first American-bred Yorkie to win AKC all-breed Best in Show in 1954.

Mary and Arthur Mills (Millbarry) imported three important dogs from England. These were Ch. Fritty, Ch. Miss Wynsum and Ch. Suprema. Ch. Miss Wynsum was the first Yorkshire to win the Toy Group at Westminster. Ch. Suprema won two Groups and sired seven champions, including Ch. Millbarry's Sho Sho, who was the second dog to win the Toy Group at Westminster. Ch. Fritty was first sold to the actress Mary Carlisle and was ultimately sold to Mrs. Fred Rice when Mary Carlisle moved to South America. He won ten Toy Groups and sired two Group winners. In 1954, Fritty was voted the mascot of the Yorkshire Terrier Club of America and was used as the model for the club's official pin, which is still proudly worn by its members today.

Mrs. Paul Durgin from Minnesota imported Pretoria Action (English and Irish Ch. Twinkle Star of Clu-Mor ex Connie of Adelaide) from Ireland in 1951. Action's daughter, Caroline of

"Smokey" is part of the War Dog Memorial exhibit. She is pictured here on a New Guinea battlefield in 1945 curled up in her owner's helmet, which also served as her bathtub.

The crossing of several terrier breeds eventually resulted in the Yorkshire Terrier.

Clonnel, was the dam of Clarkwyn Miss Debutante, Wildweir Butterscotch, and Wildweir Lollipop.

Iola Suhr Dowd from California imported Irish and American Ch. Peter of Norlaw. He was out of Little Comet of Clu-Mor, who also sired Ch. Twinkle Star of Clu-Mor. Peter is still in many pedigrees today.

Myrtle Young imported English and American Ch. Don Carlos of Progreso, and Jim Nickerson and Bud Priser of Windamere Yorkshire Terriers in Indiana imported his son, Ch. Progress of Progreso. Progress won Bests in Show in England, America, and Canada. He sired many champions including Ch. Gaytonglen Teddy of Mayfair.

The Mayfair-Barban Kennel has owned or bred many champions and has been the foundation of many present-day lines, including Johnny Robinson's famous Trivar Kennel and Doreen Hubbard's famous Yorkboro dogs. Miss Ann Seranne started Mayfair and joined with Barbara Wolferman to become Mayfair-Barban. The Mayfair line also has many dogs who contain the genes of Ch. Golden Fame, a Yorkie who was later acquired by the Wildweir Kennel of Chicago. One of the highlights of my own career includes winning Best in Specialty Show at the Bluebonnet Yorkshire Terrier Club with my Ch. Shadomountin Steppin' Up under Miss Ann Seranne. She commented that he had the most perfect dark steel-blue coat color, with the correct texture, that she had ever seen.

Of all the Yorkshire Terrier kennels in America, Wildweir is the most famous. Joan Gordon and her twin sister, the late Miss Janet Bennett, have devoted most of their lives to the breed. They were charter members of the Yorkshire Terrier Club of America, and they worked diligently for the club and for the welfare of the breed. Miss Janet Bennett was a licensed AKC judge. One of my top wins for Steppin' Up was when Janet Bennett selected from my kennel littermates Ch. Steppin' Up Stratton and Ch. Steppin' Up Sugar Frosted (Ch. Shadomountin Steppin' Up ex Perle Bavarde D'Adelaide) as Winners Dog and Winners Bitch at the 1984 National Specialty in San Francisco. This is the only time littermates have won at the National.

Almost every top Yorkshire Terrier can be traced back to Wildweir. The sisters' careful study and their investment in both time and money in developing this breed through importing and breeding selectively is unmatched throughout the world.

While growing up, Joan and Janet had Yorkshire Terriers as pets. After much study, and after the war, they embarked on developing their line. Wildweir was started in 1949. The English import Ch. Little Sir Model (ex English Ch. Ben's Blue Pride) was purchased and was the first Yorkshire Terrier to record a Best in Show. Ch. Little Sir Model was based on Pellon and Armley lines. These lines trace back to Huddersfield Ben through his grandson, Ch. Ted. Ch.

Janet Bennett is pictured here with an armful of Yorkies in 1956: Ch. Blue Velvet of Soham, Ch. Martywyn's Wee Mischief, Ch. Star Twilight of Clu-Mor, and Ch. Coulgorn Gay Lady.

Little Sir Model was bred to a bitch of Clu-Mor breeding, producing Ch. Proud Girl of Clu-Mor. She was the first bitch to win an all-breed Best in Show. She was bred to Ch. Star Twilight of Clu-Mor and produced five champions.

Ch. Little Sir Model, Ch. Golden Fame, Ch. Star Twilight of Clu-Mor, and Ch. Flook of Achmonie were Wildweir's original foundation studs. All of the dogs they subsequently imported, as well as all of their homebred champions, have been related to one or more of these original dogs.

Of all the Wildweir sires, Ch. Star Twilight of Clu-Mor was the most influential, both in the ring and as a sire. He won the Toy Group at Westminster in 1954 and 1955, the only Yorkshire Terrier to win the Group there twice. He was a beautiful and sound dog, one who could walk in the ring today and still be a top winner. He won 26 Bests in Show, 81 Groups, and 5 Specialties. He held the record for winning in the breed until Ch. Cede Higgens took over. Higgens was his great-great-grandson.

Ch. Wildweir Pomp N' Circumstance (Ch. Wildweir Cock of the Walk ex Capri Venus) was a double grandson of Ch. Star Twilight of Clu-Mor. He sired 95 champions. He appears in the background of two-thirds of all Best in Show Yorkshires at least one time.

Wildweir's most influential stud, Ch. Star Twilight of Clu-Mor, won the first Yorkshire Terrier Club of America specialty in 1954.

One Wildweir son of Pomp N' Circumstance who really made a great contribution to the breed was Champion Wildweir Fair N' Square. A top winner himself, he sired 18 champions, including Ch. Cloverwee Magic Marker, whose son, Ch. Ladylair Moonlight Magic, sired Lordean's Moonlight Lady—a top-producing bitch.

Fair N' Square was the grandsire of Ch. Trivar's Cookie Monster, Ch. Wildweir Bumper Sticker, Ch. Wildweir Respected Legend, and Ch. Cupoluv's Fair LeGrand.

My own line is basically all Wildweir breeding coming down from Pomp N' Circumstance through line-breeding on his son, Ch. Wildweir Ten O' Clock Scholar. I was able to tighten up this line by having the opportunity to breed to Ch. Wildweir Bumper Sticker. I considered this breeding to be one of the turning points in my breeding program. Ten O' Clock Scholar's dam, Wildweir Dilly Dally, was also the great-grandmother of Ch. Wildweir Bumper Sticker.

In 1979, Ch. Gleno Credit Card (ex Irish and English Ch. Blairsville Royal Seal) joined Wildweir. He sired seven champions, including Nancy Donovan's Ch. Wildweir Tabaho and Betty Dullinger's Ch. Wildweir Master Card, who in turn sired German

Careful, conscientious breeding has resulted in the many great lines of Yorkshires existing today.

Ch. Turyanne Shannon of Shamrock. Ch. Wildweir Tabaho sired Ch. Wildweir Nableca, Chip Wilson's bitch, who was Best of Opposite at Westminster.

Turyanne in Connecticut is owned by Kathleen Kolbert and Richard Lawrence. Kathleen first bred under the name Windsor, and then Windsor-Gayelyn with Marilyn Koenig. She has imported dogs based on the Millmoor line from Belgium. She is also an AKC licensed judge and has owned or bred over 90 champions. Mrs. Ila Clark from Seattle, Washington, owned Ch. Toy Clown of Rusklyn imported by Wildweir. Her foundation bitch, mentioned earlier, was bred to Ch. Wildweir Pomp N' Circumstance and produced Ch. Clarkwyn Dreamy Doll. Dreamy Doll's son, bred to Toy Clown's daughter, produced Ruth Jenkins' Ch. Clarkwyn Jubilee Eagle. Jubilee Eagle was a top producer, having produced 52 champions, including Ch. Cede Higgens, the all-time top winner of the breed and the only Yorkshire Terrier to ever win Best in Show at the Westminster Kennel Club. I personally had the opportunity to meet the breeder of Cede Higgens, Mr. C.D. Lawrence. He is a charming man and so devoted to the breed. I am privileged to have met him.

Mrs. Jenkins, who owned Ch. Clarkwyn Jubilee Eagle, has bred or owned over 55 champions. Her kennel name is Jentre. Ruth acquired the imports Ch. Wenscoe's Whizzaway of Tzumiao and his son Ch. Wenscoe's Zippadee Du Dah from Mrs. Wendy Whitely when she retired from breeding. Whizzaway sired Ch. Juana and Jentre's Blue Jeans, who produced ten champions. Besides Cede Higgens, her Jubilee Eagle sired the famous Ch. Robtell Jubilation, owned by Martell Roberts, and Ch. Jentre's Charger of Mistangay, sold to Renee Emmons. Jentre's Charger of Mistangay was the foundation for many of today's top dogs, such as the Rothby, Caraneal, and Stratford lines. Ch. Finstal Royal Icing (English import sired by Ch. Finstal Jonathan) was acquired by Mrs. Jenkins in 1984 and has sired over 30 champions. Mrs. Jenkins has certainly made a contribution to the breed through her ability to select a good dog.

Currently, there are many great lines of Yorkshires, all from the foundation laid down by these great dogs and their insightful breeders. None of these dogs are without fault, as are none of ours. However, the opportunities are boundless and the future is bright.

STANDARD for the Yorkshire Terrier

The standard for a particular dog breed describes the characteristics that make up that breed. These characteristics include the breed's purpose, personality or temperament, general appearance, structural differences that make the breed able to perform its function, and details of its "type" or "look."

The standard has been studied and approved by the breed's parent club and the national kennel club—it is a plan or a pattern for a breeder to follow. All standards assume physical and mental soundness. There are over 150 breeds currently accepted and registered with the American Kennel Club. Each breed's standard describes the dog and what sets him or her apart from all other dogs. This is what makes a Dalmatian a white dog with spots. It makes a Collie look like "Lassie." It makes a Great Dane a giant noble dog. It assures us that a toy dog will be a small dog who can sit on our lap or be carried in our arms. In other words, the standard should be a guarantee of predictability. It assures us that the puppy we see will mature to look and act as we had expected.

It is interesting to note that head type, coat color and texture, and size are important in all standards. The head is the first thing we see when we look at the animal, and because most things change in relation to one another, from here goes the rest of the dog: i.e., small, massive; short, long; refined, powerful. Most standards, after the general description, begin with the head. This sets the "type" for the rest of the dog.

The breed standard describes the characteristics that make up the breed, and it has been studied and approved by the breed's parent club.

Following the description of the head are the descriptions of coat color and texture, size, body, legs, movement, etc. All of these components make up the specific breed type. Without this "type," no matter how sound the animal, we have no way to evaluate and preserve consistency in the breed.

Here you will find the UK breed standard adopted by the Kennel Club of Great Britain in 1887 and the American standard adopted by the American Kennel Club in 1966. The two are nearly identical with the exception of a few minor points (and of course, individual interpretations).

THE KENNEL CLUB BREED STANDARD

General Appearance

Long-coated, coat hanging quite straight and evenly down each side, a parting extending from nose to end of tail. Very compact and neat, carriage very upright conveying an important air. General outline conveying impression of vigorous and well proportioned body.

The Kennel Club breed standard describes the Yorkshire Terrier as alert and intelligent, with an even, spirited disposition.

The Yorkie's body is well proportioned and very compact. The back line should be level, not sloping.

Characteristics
Alert, intelligent toy terrier.

Temperament
Spirited with even disposition.

Head and Skull
Rather small and flat, not too prominent or round in skull, nor too long in muzzle; black nose.

Eyes
Medium, dark, sparkling, with sharp intelligent expression and placed to look directly forward. Not prominent. Edge of eyelids dark.

Ears
Small, V-shaped, carried erect, not too far apart, covered with short hair, colour very deep, rich tan.

Mouth
Perfect, regular and complete scissor bite, i.e. upper teeth closely

overlapping lower teeth and set square to the jaws. Teeth well placed with even jaws.

Neck
Good reach.

Forequarters
Well-laid shoulders, legs straight, well covered with hair of rich golden tan a few shades lighter at ends than at roots, not extending higher on forelegs than elbow.

Body
Compact with moderate spring of rib, good loin. Level back.

Hindquarters
Legs quite straight when viewed from behind, moderate turn of stifle. Well covered with hair of rich golden tan a few shades lighter at ends than at roots, not extending higher on hindlegs than stifles.

Tail
Customarily docked
Docked: Medium length with plenty of hair, darker blue in colour than rest of body, especially at end of tail. Carried a little higher than level of back.
Undocked: Plenty of hair, darker blue in colour than rest of body, especially at end of tail. Carried a little higher than level of back. As straight as possible. Length to give a well-balanced appearance.

Gait/Movement
Free with drive; straight action front and behind, retaining level topline.

Coat
Hair on body moderately long, perfectly straight (not wavy), glossy; fine silky texture, not woolly. Fall on head long, rich golden tan, deeper in colour at sides of head, about ear roots, and on muzzle where it should be very long. Tan on head not to extend on to neck, nor must any sooty or dark hair intermingle with any of tan.

The Yorkshire Terrier is renowned for his small size and beautiful tan and steel-blue coat.

Colour

Dark steel blue (not silver blue), extending from occiput to root of tail, never mingled with fawn, bronze, or dark hairs. Hair on chest rich, bright tan. All tan hair darker at the roots than in middle, shading to still lighter at tips.

Size

Weight up to 3.2 kgs (7 lbs).

Faults

Any departure from the foregoing points should be considered a fault, and the seriousness with which the fault should be regarded should be in exact proportion to its degree and its effect upon the health and welfare of the dog.

Note

Male animals should have two apparently normal testicles fully descended into the scrotum.

—July 2001

The American Kennel Club standard calls for the Yorkie coat to be moderately long and straight.

THE AMERICAN KENNEL CLUB BREED STANDARD

General Appearance

That of a long-haired toy terrier whose blue and tan coat is parted on the face and from the base of the skull to the end of the tail and hangs evenly and quite straight down each side of body. The body is neat, compact, and well proportioned. The dog's high head carriage and confident manner should give the appearance of vigor and self-importance.

This Yorkie's eyes are dark and sparkling, his head is characteristically small, and his long facial furnishings are impeccably maintained.

Head

Small and rather flat on top, the *skull* not too prominent or round, the *muzzle* not too long, with the *bite* neither undershot nor overshot and teeth sound. Either scissors bite or level bite is acceptable. The *nose* is black. *Eyes* are medium in size and not too prominent; dark in color and sparkling with a sharp, intelligent expression. Eye rims are dark. Ears are small, V-shaped, carried erect and set not too far apart.

Body

Well proportioned and very compact. The back is rather short, the back line level, with height at shoulder the same as at the rump.

Legs and Feet

Forelegs should be straight, elbows neither in nor out. *Hind legs* straight when viewed from behind, but stifles are moderately bent when viewed from the sides. *Feet* are round with black toenails. Dewclaws, if any, are generally removed from the hind legs. Dewclaws on the forelegs may be removed.

Tail

Docked to a medium length and carried slightly higher than the level of the back.

The proper texture of a Yorkie's coat is fine and silky, similar to that of human hair.

Coat

Quality, texture, and quantity of coat are of prime importance. Hair is glossy, fine, and silky in texture. Coat on the body is moderately long and perfectly straight (not wavy). It may be trimmed to floor length to give ease of movement and a neater appearance, if desired. The fall on the head is long, tied with one bow in center of head, or parted in the middle and tied with two bows. Hair on muzzle is very long. Hair should be trimmed short on tips of ears and may be trimmed on feet to give them a neat appearance.

Colors

Puppies are born black and tan and are normally darker in body color, showing an intermingling of black hair in the tan until they are matured. Color of hair on body and richness of tan on head and legs are of prime importance in adult dogs, to which the following color requirements apply:

Blue: Is a dark steel-blue, not a silver-blue and not mingled with fawn, bronzy or black hairs.

Tan: All tan hair is darker at the roots than in the middle, shading to still lighter tan at the tips. There should be no sooty or black hair intermingled with any of the tan.

Color on Body

The blue extends over the body from back of neck to root of tail. Hair on tail is a darker blue, especially at end of tail.

Headfall

A rich golden tan, deeper in color at sides of head, at ear roots and on the muzzle, with ears a deep rich tan. Tan color should not extend down on back of neck.

Chest and Legs

A bright, rich tan, not extending above the elbow on the forelegs nor above the stifle on the hind legs.

Weight

Must not exceed seven pounds.

—Approved April 12, 1966

INTERPRETATION OF THE STANDARDS

General Appearance

The Kennel Club and American Kennel Club's description of the breed practically says it all. In walks this beautiful little long-coated dog whose general appearance says, "I've got it all"—the beauty of a long-coated dog, the size of a toy, and the stamina and heart of a terrier.

Head

The Kennel Club and American Kennel Club standards basically give the same description of the head, eyes, ears, and mouth. The head is small. It is flat on top with no sign of a domed or "apple-headed" skull. There is a slight stop—not an exaggerated one. It is small and pretty,

Small, pointed ears are highly prized in the Yorkshire Terrier, and the best-set ears are generally of thinner ear leather.

distinguishing it from the larger terriers in the Terrier Group, yet it is not a snub-nosed "doll face." The muzzle is not long. The nose and eye rims are black, and the eyes are of a medium size and are not to be too round or prominent. There is a keen, intelligent gleam in those eyes.

With regard to the ears, it should be noted here that early ancestors had cropped ears, and many terriers have cropped or folded ears. The small pointed ears are highly prized and are the prettiest; the best-set ears are generally of thinner ear leather. It is thick ear leather that is most prone not to stand erect.

With regard to the dog's bite, either scissors or level bite is acceptable.

Body

The Yorkshire Terrier should have a well-proportioned or square body. This means that the legs and body depth should square the body against its short back. The body should be compact with good spring of rib for heart and lung capacity and stamina. The loin should be as short as possible; this adds to agility and helps the back to remain level when in motion. The length of neck and layback of the shoulders are not mentioned in the American standard as they are in the English standard; however, they are both important for the freedom of movement and the high head carriage called for in the standard. It should be realized that layback of shoulder is most important, for with a straight shoulder the dog cannot hold his head as high as he should. The straight shoulder can also cause the back to appear long. There is a current trend toward a long-legged, long-necked Yorkshire, which is totally improper. These rangy animals become slab-sided, losing the spring of rib and compact body that have always been attributes of the breed.

Legs and Feet

The American Kennel Club's standard with regard to legs and feet is pretty self-explanatory. An animal with unsound legs will not move freely and usually will not hold the topline straight. Lack of angulation in the rear legs causes excess wear on the knees (patellas).

Tail

The Kennel Club and American Kennel Club standards allow for the tail to be docked to a medium length. Please note the words

While not a disqualification, the weight of a Yorkshire Terrier should not exceed 7 pounds.

The proper coat colors for a Yorkshire Terrier are rich, golden tan and dark steel blue.

"medium length"—most veterinarians will dock the tail much too short. If you have it docked 1/8 to 1/4 of an inch into the black where the tan meets the black on the underside of the tail, you will have the proper length. The tail will have a darker shade of blue at the tip, almost black. The set of the tail is not mentioned here, but the tail should come almost straight up from the backbone. A rounded rump with a low tail-set ruins the appearance of the topline. It is better to have the tail carried too high than too low.

Coat

The Yorkie stands alone in the demand for a coat in two metallic colors of glossy, fine, silky texture. Without good quality and texture, the coat can never achieve a beautiful, glimmering metallic shine. We are dealing with a dilution factor in the coat color. Each hair should be fine, sleek, and strong. These sleek individual hairs can reflect the light, thus giving shine to the coat. A heavy coarse hair will have a dull outer layer. A soft thin hair will be fuzzy, and it will not reflect light either. The strong silky hairs not only reflect light, but they do not mat together. Hence, the true silky coat is quite easy to grow.

If you have three threads: one of wool, one of cotton, and one of silk, the wool will break first; the cotton will break second; and the silk will nearly cut your finger before it breaks! The hair on the muzzle should be quite long. The body coat is long, without any wave to it, and it may be trimmed to floor length for ease of movement. The adult Yorkshire Terrier in the show ring should have a floor-length coat. If it is not floor length, it shows neglect on the part of the owner or the genetic inability to grow coat (i.e., texture and quantity). The hair on the ears is to be trimmed to a point. The feet should have the hair around them trimmed for ease of movement.

Color

Yorkie puppies are born black with tan points above the eyes and tan on the muzzle, chest, underside of the tail, feet, and partway up the legs. The color pattern is much like any of the black-and-tan breeds, and the puppy actually matures to a tan dog with a blue saddle. You can determine somewhat of an idea about the color by the brilliance of the tan and the texture of the puppy coat. A fluffy puppy coat is incorrect and should be penalized in a show ring. Technically, a puppy cannot be faulted on color in the ring, but he can be faulted on texture: A fluffy texture will never be blue. A puppy with a brilliant tan already showing shading at the roots on the legs will usually mature to a beautiful color of both tan and blue. A puppy already breaking on the body to light blue or silver will mature to be a light-blue or silver dog. A puppy with a wavy coat generally matures into a silver adult.

Coat color is very important, just as the quality, texture, and quantity of the coat are very important. All of these features are equally important and quite hard to separate. You cannot have proper coat color without the proper quality and texture of the coat.

The dark steel-blue color is sometimes quite controversial among both fanciers and judges. Remember that black is without any light—a black coat cannot reflect light to give the brilliance of coat as does the dark steel blue. All Yorkshire Terriers become lighter-colored with age. The blue begins as black, turns to dark steel blue, and then eventually becomes medium blue or silver. Therefore, if we have a medium-to-light blue youngster, he will become too light, too soon. The dog who retains dark-blue color for a long time is highly prized and is invaluable in a breeding program. In the very

31

old English descriptions, the color was referred to as "bright steel blue." This can perhaps give us a better description of the color: bright describing the brilliance, steel describing the hue (darkness), and blue describing the color. "Bright" was later changed to "dark," probably because the dogs were becoming too light. Some black or soft-coated dogs do change to a lighter color, even very light; however, they never achieve the brilliant blue. This type of coat is referred to as clerical gray. Once you have seen and felt a true dark steel-blue coat, you will never forget it. It is truly blue!

There are two factors of the tan that are very important: golden tan and shading. The tan is to be of a brilliant golden color, never pale or sooty (with black or brown hairs). Many refer to the tan as the "gold," and this more properly describes the color. However, the term "bright" was not deleted from the description of the tan, and the texture and color of the tan make it appear "bright." The pale tan, dark-orange tan, or sooty tan will not appear bright. The shading is quite easily discerned by looking at the roots of the hair because the pigment is more concentrated at the roots. Only the proper silky texture of each hair will allow this shading to show through.

The boundaries set forth for the tan describe the pattern for the blue saddle. If the tan comes down the neck, above the elbows, or

Color, quality, texture, and quantity are all very important components of the Yorkshire Terrier coat.

above the stifles, the saddle is lost. These tan hairs intermingled with the blue hairs give a bronze cast to the coat. The tan actually comes up behind the hind legs, around the vent, and up the underside of the tail. If this tan runs out of pattern, there will be a gold cast in front of the tail. These breaks in the tan pattern are often referred to as "running gold." A Yorkshire with a sooty tan will often have a dark streak between the eyes and on either side of the head. These are often referred to as "thumb-prints." Do not confuse dark roots of a good shaded tan for thumb-prints. Just as with the beautiful blue, the glorious shaded golden tan will never be forgotten once you have seen it.

The Yorkshire Terrier's alert expression and well-proportioned body give the dog a pleasing overall appearance.

Size

Years ago when the Kennel Club and American Kennel Club standards were written, breeders weighed their dogs and decided that on the average, they would not breed anything over 7 pounds. Although this is not a disqualification (there are no disqualifications in the Yorkshire standard), it is nonetheless key that the Yorkshire not exceed 7 pounds!

Small bitches under 3 $^3/_4$ to 4 pounds probably should not be bred for health reasons. However, I have seen quite a few 3-pound bitches free whelp puppies with no problem at all, and quite a few 7-pound bitches who had to be sectioned. In my own line, the 4 $^1/_2$- to 5-pound females have always produced the best puppies. Remember, the 7-pound bitch is likely to produce an 8- or 9-pound boy! There should be no room in anyone's breeding program for an oversized male.

CHARACTERISTICS of the Yorkshire Terrier

Although the Yorkshire Terrier is a small toy breed best known for his beautiful silken coat of blue and tan and his spunky, confident character, there are many wonderful characteristics that make this little dog so popular.

HUNTER

Most Yorkies have not lost their basic hunting instincts. They will definitely stalk, catch, and kill a mouse. They also catch bugs, snakes, frogs, and just about anything else considered fair game.

WATCHDOG

The Yorkie is also fearless as a watchdog. He has a great sense of hearing and can usually hear someone coming long before they get to the door. However, he is not prone to being a yippy little dog who barks for no reason.

Yorkshire Terriers love to spend time with their families, and they adapt easily to all types of living quarters.

Yorkshire Terriers make wonderful family pets, and they are extremely devoted to their human companions.

Although Yorkies are great watchdogs, they seldom bark without some kind of provocation.

Some Yorkshires can be quite aggressive toward strange dogs. They must be watched carefully! Many a little Yorkie has met his demise by attacking a larger dog.

HUMAN COMPANION

Yorkshire Terriers are very devoted to their owners. Most will prefer to share your bed if you will allow it. They are quite agile, and they will stay out of the way of your feet—just a few little bumps and they learn to watch for you. When we have puppies at our house, we call our gait "the puppy shuffle" as we scoot our feet to push the puppies out of the way rather than step on them.

The Yorkshire Terrier might not be for you if you require a very obedient dog, because this dignified, playful, feisty, sweet little dog cannot be made to do anything he makes up his mind not to do! Some Yorkies take to correction better than others, but it usually works out best if you use positive training methods.

Yorkshire Terriers are the easiest long-coated dogs to care for because they have single silken coats that do not shed.

The role of toy breeds in modern society has a very bright future. These small dogs make excellent personal companions. They adapt easily to all types of living quarters, be it a country home or a small apartment. Therefore, should it be necessary to move, it is not a major problem for the dog. Many retirement homes and communities now welcome small dogs. One of my Yorkies now resides in a nursing home in Arkansas. She belongs to the owner and has free run of the facility, complete with a doggie-door to the courtyard area. Several puppies have even been acquired by retired persons traveling the country in motor homes.

The Yorkshire Terrier is a great pet for a single person or a couple. He can also make a good family pet if the children are responsible and kind to animals. It is not fair to place a small dog with children who might be unkind to him. The dog could be injured, could become afraid, or could become aggressive and possibly bite the children. If you have children and decide that the Yorkshire is the breed that you want, a larger, more outgoing male puppy will make a great family pet.

Finally, you must consider coat care. Of all the long-coated breeds of dog, the Yorkshire is the easiest to care for because he has a single coat (no undercoat) of silken texture. The coat is much like human hair. Yorkies do not shed or blow coat. You will find a few hairs around the house or have hair in their hairbrushes, much like your own hair. If kept indoors and bathed weekly, Yorkies should not bother allergy sufferers. If you are not interested in the long coat, they are just as adorable with cute shorter haircuts.

SELECTING a Yorkshire Terrier

F irst of all, before buying any dog—do your homework! This little creature will be your companion and friend for maybe 10 to 15 years. You want to find the right dog for you. If you think about it, the time and money spent now will pay off in the future. You want your Yorkshire to suit you in looks and in personality. The initial expense of buying a dog is a fraction of what you will spend on the animal in his lifetime. You will have food, grooming, and veterinary expenses, as well as expenses for little luxuries for your dog.

I would recommend that you attend some dog shows and see the dogs being shown. Which ones appeal to you? Visit with some exhibitors, if possible, after they are finished showing. It takes a lot of grooming and mental preparation for both owner and dog before showing. Many a prospective owner goes away from a show feeling that the exhibitors were rude, when possibly they were just busy getting ready. Showing is a very competitive sport, and exhibitors want every hair in place; they also want their little athletes to be physically and mentally prepared for the short time they have to "show off." After showing, they can go back to their setup or benching areas to relax and have some conversation.

Buy books and read as much as you can about the breed before you buy the dog. Don't get the dog and then the book! The little puppies you see are not going to look anything like the older dogs you see at the show. You will need to know what the puppies look like and what you can expect to see in their development.

FINDING A BREEDER

First, find yourself a mentor if you can. A reputable breeder can be found. As I mentioned earlier, visit shows and talk to other Yorkshire owners before making any decisions. You may contact the American Kennel Club, which can put you in touch with the secretary of the Yorkshire Terrier Club of America. The secretary, in turn, can refer you to a breed club or a breeder in your area. If there is an all-breed kennel club in your city, they often have a list of good breeders. If a breeder does not have any puppies, you may get on a waiting list, or he or she may know someone else who currently has puppies.

Expect your breeder to ask questions. He or she will want to know if you want a show dog or a pet. There are many very nice puppies who have small faults that may keep them from being show dogs. A good breeder will be honest with you as to what these faults might be. Maybe the puppy will be too large or too small for breeding. Maybe the breeder does not want to keep a male at this time. You can usually acquire a good male more easily than a female, as breeders must be most particular in the males they keep.

Don't ask for a show dog if you don't plan to show him, as it is very disappointing for a breeder to sell a good-quality show dog if the dog will never have a chance in the ring.

Your breeder may ask questions about your home, your lifestyle, and your family. Don't be offended, as breeders want the best for their puppies and want you and the puppy to be happy.

By the same token, you should feel free to ask questions about the puppy, his parents, and the way he has been raised and handled. Ask if you may see the parents. Sometimes the sire may be elsewhere because the bitch was bred to a dog across the country, but the

When selecting a Yorkshire puppy, evaluate the cleanliness of both the dog and the area in which he and his littermates are being kept.

Before purchasing your Yorkshire puppy, research the breed and determine whether it is the right one for your family's lifestyle.

Most Yorkshire Terrier puppies will grow to be a little more than double their weight by the time they are 12 weeks of age.

breeder will have his picture and pedigree. Most good breeders sell their pet puppies "not for breeding."

DECIDING TO BREED

The breeding of dogs requires a lot of time and commitment, and Yorkshire Terriers are not very easily bred by novices. The little female requires constant monitoring as whelping time nears. She will probably require some assistance with the birth. All usually goes well; however, veterinary assistance or a cesarean section is always a possibility. The puppies usually weigh between 3 and 6 ounces at birth, so you might be spending several sleepless nights with your new family. With the costs of stud fees, feeding, veterinary care, and vaccinations, you probably will not make a profit. If you should decide to breed, find a good breeder to help you select the bitch as well as the male to whom she should be bred. You will also need to have a very good veterinarian. There are also many good books available on genetics and dog breeding.

I sell all of my pet puppies with "limited" registrations, which means the dog may not be shown in conformation, and the puppies from that dog may not be registered. The dog is eligible for obedience and all other AKC events, such as tracking and agility. It is my theory that if the dog is not of quality to show, he is not of quality to breed. In thinking this way, we can try to improve the show quality of our breed and produce excellent quality pet dogs as well. We are faced with an overpopulation of dogs and cats. You will rarely find a Yorkshire Terrier in an animal shelter, and I hope we can keep it this way.

PICKING A PUPPY

The best age at which to evaluate Yorkshire Terrier puppies for pet or for show is 12 weeks. At this magical time, everything begins to come together. If you have studied the standard, you may see the crucial elements begin to emerge that set this breed apart from all others.

Size

At this time, you may predict the size of the adult dog. A good rule of thumb is to double the weight at 12 weeks. I have found this to be pretty accurate, with a few exceptions. Most puppies, unless they are extremely chubby, will grow to be a little more than double their weight at 12 weeks. A puppy that weighs in at 2 pounds at 12 weeks will most likely be the perfect size. An adult dog under 4 pounds is considered to be tiny. And of course, an adult dog over 7 pounds is oversized. Compare the bones of the front legs of the litter. You should be able to determine if the dog will be fine boned or coarse.

At 12 weeks, the Yorkshire puppy may be slightly longer in back than tall. He will soon have a growth spurt and gain some height. The adult dog should appear to be square, with the length of back in relation to the height at the shoulders.

Form

The topline should be perfectly level. Any dips or humps at this age will more than likely not go away. Stand the puppy on a table or on the floor and feel down the back for any dips behind the shoulders or rolls over the loin. A short loin is highly desirable. A long, narrow loin will later show up to be a roached (curved) topline, particularly if there is not enough angulation in the rear end. A dip behind the point where the shoulders come together will probably never go away.

After 12 weeks, the level topline may "go off" once or twice as the puppy grows. However, if it was good at 12 weeks, it will usually come back. I have found that this happens to the puppies with the best angulation more often than to puppies with no angulation, only to come back as perfect. A dog with poor angulation in the rear and/or with long hocks will likely go "high" in the rear.

Shoulder placement and angulation are extremely important in the Yorkshire Terrier, for it is the layback of the shoulder and not the length of the neck that give the Yorkie his high head carriage. A dog with poor layback finds his withers in his neck, and the poor thing must move with his head down or with his neck bowed in a ewe position.

I'd like to make a note here about length of neck. Currently, there is a trend toward Yorkies with the long-necked and long-legged "elegant" look. Unfortunately, you cannot change the number of vertebrae. Everything eventually changes in proportion. Therefore, the dogs will also develop long muzzles and long backs that are lean and narrow.

The Yorkshire Terrier is a compact little dog. He should have a solid, broad body with good depth and breadth of chest. This gives

Yorkshire Terriers should only be bred by those who are experienced and committed to the betterment of the breed.

plenty of room for the heart and lungs. If the body is lean, the pelvic area is usually narrow, and this will cause the rear to be too close. The dog's rear movement may cause him to appear as though he is moving with one leg in the rear.

The Yorkie's front legs should be straight, with the elbows fitting close to the body. Having evolved from the digging terrier family, the front feet sometimes turn out slightly. The back legs should have short hocks and be parallel from behind. There should be moderate angulation to the rear at stifle and hock when viewed from the side. Hopefully, the angulation of rear and front will match, as this is essential for the level back. A dog with poor angulation in the rear can still have a level topline if the front angles are also straight. This dog will lack reach and drive and will move with a choppy, rough stride. Straight stifles are very hard on the kneecaps because they serve as "shock absorbers." Luxating patellas (dislocating kneecaps) are quite common in all toy dogs. This is usually caused by lack of angulation in the rear, poor muscle development, and jumping. This can become quite uncomfortable to the dog, causing pain and arthritis in later years. Sometimes the condition warrants surgery. Ask your veterinarian to check the patellas of your new puppy. This should be done gently. The kneecaps should never be forced out of place! Every time the kneecap "pops" out of place, the tendons and ligaments become more and more stretched. Remember, this little kneecap is probably smaller than the nail on your pinky finger.

Head and Facial Features

The Yorkshire Terrier puppy should have a pretty face with very dark, medium-sized eyes. Remember, the Kennel Club and American Kennel Club standards say that the head is small and rather flat on top. Smooth the hair back on the top to see if the top of the skull is rather flat. A domed skull is not only improper, it is indicative of hydrocephalus, a deadly condition which causes seizures. The eye of a hydrocephalic puppy will have a pushed-in look caused by pressure within the skull. This condition is not common, but it can occur. It is often accompanied by a large soft spot or open fontanel in the skull. Again, ask your veterinarian to look for this when he checks the puppy. Extreme baby-doll faces are prone to this condition.

The nose, eye rims, and lips of the puppy should be black. There should be no discharge from the eyes, nose, or mouth. The teeth should meet in a level or scissors bite. There should be six incisors between the canines (sharp teeth), top and bottom. Missing teeth here can be indicative of other missing teeth and can cause bite problems when the puppy later gets his permanent teeth. In an older puppy, be cautious of a double set of teeth (retained puppy teeth). Sometimes the puppy teeth aren't pushed out properly by the emerging adult teeth. These must be removed by a skillful hand and will sometimes require a veterinarian. Be sure to have any retained puppy teeth removed at the time of neutering.

Hold the puppy and look at the angle at which the muzzle comes out from between the eyes. Although the Yorkie should not have a lot of stop or definition as the muzzle meets the foreskull, the muzzle should come straight out from below the eyes. A down angle to the face, referred to as "down-faced," is not very attractive. Muzzle lengths vary from long to short. Muzzle widths range from very broad to snipy or pointed. Beauty here may lie in the eye of the beholder. Again, the standard says the head is small and rather flat on top, and the muzzle is not too long. I think the key word here is *small*. The head is small in proportion to the body. Your Yorkie should be a true, smart-looking little terrier with no signs of coarseness.

A Yorkshire Terrier puppy should have a pretty face with dark, medium-sized eyes; the head should be small and rather flat on top.

At this point, we must look at the ears. Of all the long-coated, "beautiful" breeds, the Yorkshire Terrier is the only one with erect, or "up," ears. The ears can make or break the expression. The ears are "small, V-shaped...not too far apart." Large or widely set ears ruin the look of the head. A 12-week-old puppy should have his ears "up." If they aren't up by this age, they may never come up. Often, the ear-set will improve with age. The size of the ears may appear smaller as the facial furnishings grow. However, they do keep growing as the body grows. The ears are trimmed about halfway down and should be trimmed to a point. Be sure the hair is always trimmed on a puppy's ears from the time he is two weeks old. The weight of the hair can keep the ears from coming up and can cause them to come down or tip over at the top.

Tail

The tail should be docked to a medium length and carried higher than the back line. The Yorkshire Terrier, at attention, should bring the tail upright. When the dog is moving, the tail should be visible above the back. The tail-set, where it comes away from the body, is very important. The tail should come straight off the top of the back. A low tail-set is not proper and ruins the appearance of the topline.

Coat

The coat is the most specific and the most important aspect of the Yorkshire Terrier for show purposes. The glorious metallic blue and gold colors of silken hair are the essence of breed type in the Yorkie. Even if you are choosing your dog as a companion, you want to acquire the best coat you can. The proper texture of pure silk is easy to maintain because it does not mat.

There are several types of puppy coats that actually turn out quite nicely. Different lines develop in different ways. Therefore, your breeder may be able to help you. Ask the breeder how the coat will develop. In my line, I know pretty well what to expect from the puppy coat. However, I might be in doubt when dealing with an outcross breeding. When in doubt, I would ask the owner of the sire how his line develops.

The coat of a puppy should be sleek, shiny, and perfectly black, almost blue-black. The black should dilute to dark steel blue. A fluffy puppy coat may be awfully cute, but it will not develop into

The coat color and texture of your prospective Yorkshire Terrier puppy is important if you plan to show him.

the silky, glossy coat that it should. It will be either cottony or woolly. Often, the skimpiest puppy coat will mature into a beautiful adult coat. Fluffy tan legs are a dead giveaway to an improper adult coat.

There are several types of head color on puppies. The puppy may have sparse hair on the head with a very bright gold coming in at the roots. This will usually be a perfect golden tan as an adult. Sometimes this type of head color will retain a little dark area between the eyes and on each side of the head until maturity. These little spots on either side of the head are referred to as "thumbprints."

Another type of head color on puppies occurs when the entire head changes at the roots from black to almost white or silver. This, too, will be a beautiful golden tan at maturity. It will become richer in color as the dog matures and will usually, though not always, be shaded. This type of head coloring often appears on a dog who will be silver as an adult.

When the head has a dull tan color or a dark orange or brown mixed with black, you may have a tan that will never clear itself of the black. I think the key here is to look for brightness around the muzzle and over the eyes where the tan was as a newborn. Beware of a dull, murky look to the head.

Look at the puppy's legs. Many breeders and exhibitors first check the tan on the legs. Again, fluffy legs are indicative of a soft or woolly coat texture. The coats that mature to be the most perfect will show shading at the roots of the leg hair first. This is highly prized in a puppy.

Temperament

In selecting a puppy for a pet or for show, the temperament, or personality, is one of the most important aspects. Does the puppy seem happy with his littermates? Does he wag his tail when you talk to him? Is he afraid of you? Does he have his tail up when he walks? These are important things to note.

Think of your lifestyle and the personality of the dog you want to own. Do you want a pretty little pet who is very sweet and loving, or do you want a feisty extrovert who greets everyone gregariously? There is a great difference in these two personalities. That outgoing personality might be great in the show ring, but will he be a bit too much to live with? By the same token, you don't want a dog who spends most of his time hiding under the bed! Most people are happier with a dog who falls somewhere in between these two

When selecting a puppy for pet or for show, temperament is one of the most important criteria you should consider.

categories. Sometimes a slightly reserved dog comes out of his shell when he becomes someone's special friend. Remember, the puppy does not know you. Check how he reacts to the breeder. Dogs transfer their affections quite easily. The puppy will probably act much the same toward you as he acts with his current owner.

I would never accept a Yorkshire Terrier who is trembling or who shies away; this is just not characteristic of the breed. He may not come running to you because he doesn't know you, so watch how he reacts to his surroundings.

Most puppies acquired from breeder exhibitors have a stable temperament. A breeder exhibitor begins socializing puppies from birth. Show dogs are accustomed to traveling, crowds, other breeds, handling by strangers, grooming, etc. Any hereditary tendency toward shyness is quickly eliminated from a line of show dogs. Ask the breeder his opinion of the dog's personality. I personally like a dog who makes eye contact with me.

ADOPTING AN OLDER DOG

Perhaps you don't want to raise a puppy. An older dog might be a better option for you if you don't care to go through puppyhood.

Puppies require much more time and patience, almost like their human counterparts. The puppy requires almost constant supervision, several meals per day, housetraining, leash training, etc. Sometimes an older dog can be found through a breeder or a rescue organization. You will definitely see what you are getting; however, the growing of the coat will be up to you. I place my females when they are around five years old. Since Yorkies live to be quite old, they make wonderful pets for many years. I choose the homes very carefully, and the dogs always go out on a trial basis. In all the years, there has only been one placement that didn't work out. The lady said the dog wasn't happy. It turned out the dog had an ear infection!

A local breed club can sometimes help you find an adult dog. There might be a nice young adult who just didn't make it for show. Sometimes a breeder must find a good home for an adult dog to make room for upcoming young stars.

When purchasing a puppy or an adult, make certain to obtain the registration slip or a bill of sale naming the dog's sire, dam, registration number, and date of birth. Make certain you have time to have the dog checked by a veterinarian. Obtain a list of the dog's vaccinations and any medications he may have taken, including wormers. Get a list of feeding instructions. Make certain all

If you don't have the time to devote to training a puppy, then adopting an older dog might be a better option.

If you are looking for an older dog, your local breed club may be able to assist you in the process.

Spaying or neutering your Yorkshire Terrier will help eliminate many health problems and behavioral issues.

conditions of the sale, if any, are understood and in writing. Don't hesitate to call the breeder if any questions arise.

THE IMPORTANCE OF SPAYING AND NEUTERING

You will find your pet will be a much better pet if he or she is neutered or spayed. You won't be troubled with the female coming into season twice a year and having to be confined. She won't have breast tumors or uterine problems as an older pet. Your little male won't be slipping out the door to roam down the street looking for a girlfriend. Neutering also eliminates urine marking, and contrary to what some people think, both dogs and bitches who are sexually intact will usually mark their territory! You will have a healthier, happier pet if it is neutered. This should usually be done before sexual maturity, so discuss this with your veterinarian. A word of caution, though: Please be sure your veterinarian is aware that a Yorkshire Terrier must be treated with extreme caution when receiving any form of anesthetic.

CARING for Your Yorkshire Terrier

Before you take your puppy home, you will need to purchase a crate in which to carry him. Decide where your puppy will sleep. It is best to confine him to one area, preferably with tile or linoleum. You can buy a bed for him, or you can make one from a cardboard carton cut down on one side, with a piece of soft blanket inside. He will need a place to call his own. You may want to purchase a couple of toys; Nylabone® products are good for puppies due to their softer composition. It also doesn't hurt to have some newspaper on the floor in case of an accident.

HOUSEHOLD DANGERS

There are many dangers around the house for a small puppy. Electrical cords are a real danger, because if he should chew through one it could mean a severe shock, a burn to the mouth, or even death. You can buy a bitter spray to apply to things he shouldn't chew, but a very sharp "no" will help him learn! Be careful about small objects on the floor, such as plants, chemicals, and especially pills. It is not safe to take your puppy to public places or to let

Before you bring your new Yorkshire Terrier puppy home, it's a good idea to purchase a crate, such as the Nylabone® Fold-Away Pet Carrier.

him socialize with other dogs until he has completed his puppy vaccinations. This is usually after 16 weeks, and your veterinarian can advise you about this. A word of caution: Young puppies can have a reaction to the leptospirosis vaccine. I give the "puppy shot" vaccine, which is a combination vaccine without leptospirosis, when the dog is older.

HANDLING

It's important that you always keep a finger around one of your Yorkie's front legs when carrying him. The curious, wiggly little fellow can leap or fall in the blink of an eye. When a visitor picks up your dog, always caution him to hold on to the dog. Your puppy can decide he's had enough and bail out at any moment. Always insist that children sit on the floor to hold your Yorkie. If something happens, he won't have far to fall.

HOUSETRAINING

Your puppy will not come automatically housetrained. This will take time and patience. Remember, a puppy is like a baby; he has very little control. He must learn what is expected of him, and it should be taught in a kind and encouraging way. The puppy should not have free run of the house without supervision until he is housetrained. Even if you are acquiring an older dog, it is advisable to keep him confined to one area until he knows what is expected. Some people like to purchase a small wire pen or build a wooden playpen for the dog. This is not cruel if he has plenty of love and attention and plenty of playtime and exercise.

Housetraining a dog can be compared to toilet training a child. It is not fun or easy, but it is necessary for the happiness and cleanliness of all concerned. A puppy, like a human child, has little control at first. As I previously mentioned, it is a good idea to confine the puppy to a tile floor or to purchase a pen. Depending on the age of the puppy and the outdoor weather conditions, you may first want to paper-train the puppy. A puppy will not soil his bed, so you can start out with newspapers spread out on a large area, then narrow it down gradually to the place you want him to use, perhaps a corner or by the door. I never take young puppies outdoors before they are vaccinated for fear they might be exposed to something. Only after all their shots are complete do I take them outside. Paper-training always comes in handy later in life for trips and really bad weather.

When housetraining your Yorkie, take him outside and show him where to eliminate; then, praise and reward him for eliminating in the desired location.

When you begin to take your dog outdoors, it is good idea to go out with him to the preferred spot. When he goes, be sure to praise him. It won't take long for him to figure out what is expected. Be sure to put him out first thing in the morning, after naps, and after meals. Watch him for sniffing the floor or walking in a circle with his head down, looking for a place to go. There will be a few accidents, so be sure to clean and disinfect the areas where the accidents occur. A puppy will only have a small amount of urine, so it is very easy to clean. Never scold him unless you catch him "in the act." It won't do any good after the fact; it will only confuse him. All of your efforts will be well rewarded when you have a clean, well-behaved dog.

FEEDING AND NUTRITION

Most breeders will provide you with some of the puppy's regular food. If possible, find out in advance what to feed your puppy so you can find out where to purchase the same food. It is not a good idea to change his diet at first. If you must change his food, do it gradually by mixing the regular food with the new food so you won't have an abrupt change.

Always feed a Yorkshire Terrier a very high-quality food. There are many good dog foods on the market. Leave balancing the diet to the experts! It is very difficult to balance a ration, especially for a 5-pound animal. I know your Yorkie will eventually talk you out of some of your food, but try to stick to giving him dog food. A 2-pound puppy must have a balanced diet! Ask the breeder what type of dish the puppy is using for food and for water. A young puppy should be fed three or four times a day. Most adult Yorkies like to eat twice a day.

Hypoglycemia is a condition that can occur in very young puppies. If a puppy doesn't eat for a long period of time or if he has played especially hard, he can become hypoglycemic. He may become weak, start to stagger, or even start to lose consciousness. I have seen a hypoglycemic puppy have a seizure. Basically, the puppy has run out of energy. If this happens to your puppy, quickly put some honey or syrup in his mouth. Sugar will even work if nothing else is at hand. The puppy should soon be okay and should be offered food within 15 to 20 minutes. What happens is that the puppy's blood sugar level becomes too low. Once you have brought the sugar level up, the puppy will need more nourishment or his sugar level can crash back down. This is not a common problem, but it can happen and it can be deadly. If the puppy does not react quickly, you should get to a veterinarian immediately. If this happens more than once, consult your breeder or your veterinarian for feeding advice. If you have more than one dog or cat, always separate them for feeding so you can monitor their individual eating habits.

GROOMING

Brushing

Begin to groom your puppy as soon as you bring him home. You will need a good brush of pure bristle or nylon and bristle combination; a good metal comb with coarse, fine teeth; a pair of good scissors; and a pair of dog nail clippers. Mix about 1 teaspoon of hair conditioner with water in a spray bottle. Make sure the bottle sprays a very fine mist. Then, lay the puppy on his back in your lap. He may resist, so be gentle but firm. Mist lightly and brush the coat, starting with the chest, then the legs, and then up the sides of the body and neck. If you find a tangle, work it apart with your fingers from the ends of the coat toward the body, then brush the tangle apart.

The sooner you start grooming your Yorkie, the sooner both of you will become accustomed to the routine. A fine-toothed comb is an essential grooming tool.

Turn the puppy right side up, either on your lap or on a table (hang onto him on the table so he can't jump), and brush through the coat from the neck to the tail on each side. Brush his rear end and make sure there is no dried matter caught in the hair. You may want to trim a small amount of hair around the anus for cleanliness.

Turn him to face you and brush the face, neck, and chest. Be very careful around the eyes. You may need to clean around the eye area with a moist cotton pad. Now you may take your comb and part off a small section of hair above the eyes and near the outside corners. Make a small "V" shape back toward the ears. Fasten this hair with a small latex band (bought at a dog supply store or from an orthodontist) or a small barrette. The hair may not be long enough for this until the puppy is five or six months old. Make sure the hair is not pulled too tight. To release the tension, ease the band backward a little, then push it forward.

There are several types of bows for a Yorkshire. You can tie a bow around the topknot, or you can purchase a bow that is already fastened to a barrette or a latex band. These are easily attached. The puppy may wear the bow, or he may take it off and tear it up. In time, he will become accustomed to the topknot.

Using your comb, part the hair on the dog's back, from the base of the skull down the neck and back to the tail. Brush the coat down, then run the comb through it.

Depending on the texture and quality of the coat, you may need to brush your dog every day, or you may only have to do it every few days.

Bathing

In order to have a beautiful, healthy coat, I would recommend weekly bathing. Many have asked the best way to grow the coat, and I usually say that the best remedy is soap and water. The Yorkshire Terrier's coat is very much like human hair. Clean hair and skin promote a healthy coat. Daily brushing of a dirty coat snaps the ends off. Most show dogs never go out in the grass and dirt. They are exercised on a concrete patio exercise area or on a wooden deck that can be easily cleaned. Therefore, if your pet romps outside in the yard, he will pick up a lot of dirt. Sometimes the coat gets damp from the morning dew. When you brush this dirty hair, you break it off; this is the reason for misting the coat with water and conditioner. If your dog is dirty, wash him, and you will find that

Your Yorkie will eventually become accustomed to his topknot, and there are several types of bows available that can be attached to it.

brushing out the coat is much easier. A pet in full coat can be kept beautiful with a weekly bath, which takes less than one hour, and a few minutes of brushing each day.

Because of the unique nature of the Yorkie's coat, some human hair products work perfectly. Select a dog shampoo carefully, with mildness in mind. Always use a conditioner following the shampoo. Be sure to scrub the ears and tail as they are sometimes the most oily areas of the skin. Be gentle with the rest of the coat, washing in a downward motion in the same direction as the hair grows.

If you have a spray attachment in your sink or tub, it is much easier. Wet the coat, apply the shampoo, and rinse. Repeat this if

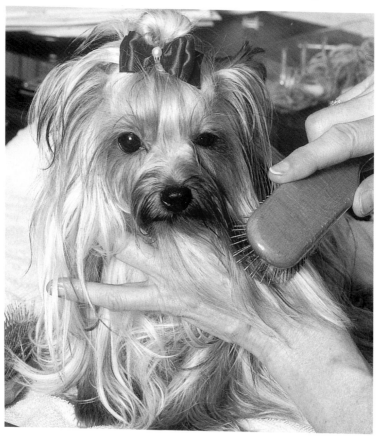

You may need to brush your dog every day or only every few days depending on the texture and quality of his coat.

Bathing your Yorkshire Terrier once a week will give him a beautiful, healthy coat.

necessary. Apply conditioner, then rinse again. You may wish to mix one teaspoon to one tablespoon of conditioner in a 16-ounce bottle of warm water and pour this over the dog as a final "leave-in" conditioner. Try different products to see what works best with your dog. Just as humans have different hair textures, thicknesses, and levels of dryness or oiliness, so do Yorkshire Terriers.

To dry the dog, wrap him in a big soft towel to soak up as much of the water as possible. You may even want to use two towels. Do not rub the coat.

You will also need a dryer. A dog stand dryer is preferable, but you can use your hair dryer stuck in a coffee can or held with a clamp. Lay the dog in your lap on his back and dry just as you brush the coat, underside and legs first, then turn him upright in your lap or on a table to dry the top of the coat. If there are tangles, work them apart with your fingers, then with the brush. Hold your hand between the mat and the body so as not to hurt the dog. Hopefully, your dog has a silk coat and your brush will just glide through the coat. Brush from the roots to the tips of the hair in long strokes. Most dogs actually love to be brushed.

If your dog has a poor coat texture, you may need to purchase a slicker brush, which has tiny wire bristles to work out the mats. Buy the gentle type and don't use it against the skin. If your Yorkshire gets to be a real mess due to a poor coat or your neglect, you may have to cut out some of the tangles or give him a cute haircut.

Ear Care

At least once a week, clean the ears with an ear cleaner and a cotton pad. If you find the ears to be very dirty or to have an odor, have your veterinarian check for ear mites or infection.

Keep the hair on the dog's ears trimmed. You may use small clippers or you may trim the hair by folding the ear over and scissoring the hair off. Trim the hair about one-third of the way down from the point of the ear, then trim each side of the ear edge from the place you trimmed toward the tip to form a point. This needs to be done at least every two weeks on puppies to be sure that the ears will stand erect. The weight of the hair can pull the ears down.

Carefully dry your Yorkie with a towel, without rubbing the coat, to soak up as much water as possible before drying him with the hair dryer.

Nail Care

Trim the hair around the feet for neatness. Trim the hair between the pads and clip the nails about every other week. Keeping the nails short will keep the dog from scratching out his coat and will make a prettier foot. Have some styptic powder available in case you cut the quick (a blood vessel which runs through the dog's nail), because it will bleed. Keeping the nails short helps to recede the quick, and you will have less chance of cutting it.

Pet Trims

There are several cute hairdos for pets. Depending

Your Yorkie's nails should be clipped approximately every other week. Nail trimming will prevent your pet from scratching out his coat and will make the foot neater.

on your lifestyle, your pet's lifestyle, and his type of coat, you may choose to give him a haircut. A few options are:

- Long coat on the body with the head hair scissored.
- The blue hair clipped off with the tan scissored.
- A total clip-down, usually only used on an older dog or one with a very poor coat.
- My favorite clip is the Westie trim. The dog is trimmed in the same way as the West Highland White Terrier. I don't care for the Schnauzer trim as it makes the Yorkshire's ears look too big.

For the Westie trim:
- With electric clippers and a medium or #8 blade, clip away all the blue coat. Here you will really notice the saddle pattern of the dog.
- Clip the neck, chest, and from below the tail down the back end to the hock. Leave the hair on the front part of the back leg.

Coat oil is often used on show dogs to protect their coats and to prevent matting and tangling.

- You may leave all the tan hair on the legs or you can feather it up a bit with scissors. Trim around the feet.
- For the head, comb a small section above the eyes forward, and trim these bangs quite short. Part the hair from the outside corner of the eyes back, and gather up the hair like you were making a ponytail from all the hair on the top of the head. With one cut of the scissors, cut up and back at an angle from the bangs. Let the hair fall and it forms a pretty layered cut around the face and head.
- For the whiskers and face fall, you can either leave them long or around the face like a Westie.
- Trim the ears normally, only taking off the hair one-third of the way down from the tip and trimming to a point.
- Trim the tan under the body from the side between the front and back legs at an angle, leaving it long near the front legs and cutting up at an angle from the front to the flank.

Another option for the head is to leave the ponytail and all of the facial furnishings while clipping off the body coat.

You may need to have the haircut done at a grooming shop if you are not proficient with electric clippers. Unlike a Poodle, the Yorkshire only needs several haircuts per year and you have the

Growing floor-length facial furnishings and a side coat past the floor requires that you wrap your Yorkie's coat.

option of growing the coat back at any time. Do not be shy in telling the groomer exactly how you want it trimmed!

Cultivating the Show Coat

As I mentioned earlier, the Yorkshire Terrier is probably the easiest of the long-coated breeds to maintain. The Yorkshire's silken coat is not prone to matting. It is a single coat. It is impossible to grow a full "specials coat" without wrapping or crackering; however, class dogs and young dogs can be done without full wraps.

Oiling

I have always kept my show dogs in coat oil. The oil keeps each individual hair coated and protected, and it also prevents matting. For oiling the coat, I mix 1 teaspoon to 1 tablespoon of coat oil (depending upon the coat texture and quantity of hair) and 1 teaspoon of conditioner with warm water in a 16-ounce bottle and pour it over the dog as a final rinse. The dog is placed in a small wire crate with a warm (not hot) dryer blowing on him for about ten minutes until damp-dry. Then I dry him as I normally would, using a nylon and bristle brush. Dogs kept in oil must be bathed weekly! Oil can clog skin pores, and it also attracts dirt. A young dog kept in coat oil only takes around 30 minutes to bathe if done weekly. If you wait two weeks, you may spend two hours removing the oil. I have found that young dogs kept in oil with the topknot, whiskers, and tail banded with fine latex bands easily grow floor-length coats. If you use this technique, don't do a lot of brushing; remember, brushing dirty hair snaps the ends right off. If the dog gets dirty, I just bathe him and then brush him out while he is still damp. Young males may need a wrap on each side, and bitches may need their skirts wrapped.

Wrapping or Crackering

In order to grow floor-length facial furnishings and a side coat past the floor, you must wrap the dog's coat.

There are many ideas for wrappers. You can use waxed paper or rice papers, which come in various colors and materials. I have always used the small deli wraps, which are thin papers waxed on one side. They are 6" x 10" and come in a box with 1,000 sheets.

Wrap the coat by parting the hair in sections, making certain the wraps do not deter free movement. The wraps should be snug but not tight. Fold the top of the wrap down about 1/2 inch and fold it

Misting and brushing your Yorkie's coat will help straighten it and remove any wrinkles after the wrappers are taken out.

in half or thirds vertically, with the top fold to the outside. Place a parted off section inside the wrapper, folding the paper around the hair. Hold the hair firmly in the wrapper near the body, fold again vertically, and then fold up or under two times and secure it with a rubber band (size #8 works well).

Wrap the topknot in one wrap (or band it with several bands), the chin whisker in one wrap and each side whisker in one wrap. The hair on the side of the head is parted from behind the ear up to just under the middle of the eye. The neck has one wrap on each side, then one on the shoulder, and one or two in the mid-section between the legs. The hip has one wrap and the leg below has one wrap; this is parted at the stifle. The tail has one wrap, and the chest area has one or two.

Some people take each wrap down and rewrap it every day. I prefer to just change the wraps as needed. Never neglect a dog in wraps. If something is amiss, fix it right away! A dangling wrapper will break the coat faster than anything. Be sure to check the underside of the wraps to see if the dog is scratching. A little satin jacket can be put on the dog over the wrappers.

You may put booties over the hind feet to deter scratching. These are usually made of tube gauze and taped at the top. I prefer to just keep the nails trimmed very short.

GROOMING FOR THE SHOW

For showing, the coat needs to be scrupulously clean, with every trace of coat oil removed. I use a grease-cutting dishwashing liquid for the first wash, then a moisturizing shampoo and a good creme rinse or conditioner for the second wash. Use plenty of water to rinse out every trace of shampoo.

For the show, start to dry your dog when he is wet, not damp, and use a warmer dryer than the one you use for weekly grooming. Brush each area until completely dry. After drying the underside, dry the flank area and tail to make certain that each hair dries perfectly straight. If you need to wrap the coat, wrap it rather loosely so the wrinkles are easier to remove.

Make certain that the dog's coat does not deter his movement. Trim the coat by placing the dog near the edge of a table, brushing the coat down, and trimming just below the edge of the table.

When you get to the show, take the dog's wraps out and straighten the coat by misting and brushing. You can purchase an electric straightening iron that works perfectly. Next, put up your topknot and tie on the bow. You should practice your topknots at home. The parting and the placement for each dog will be different. You can also experiment with different sizes and colors of bows—most Yorkshires look best in red bows. After the dog's topknot is in place, you can put on the lead and you and your Yorkie will be ready to go! All of your efforts come together right here.

There is a current trend for overexaggerated topknots and tying the hair on the ears into the topknot to hold up the ears. These topknots give the Yorkshire a hydrocephalic look. Remember that the Kennel Club and American Kennel Club standards call for the head to be small and rather flat, with the muzzle not too long. If you have a wide ear-set or a long muzzle, you should breed it out, not groom it out. These practices will only hurt the breed in the long run. You won't fool any judge worth his salt, and you will be the loser in your breeding program.

DENTAL CARE for Your Yorkshire Terrier

Anyone who has ever raised a puppy is abundantly aware of how the arrival of a new puppy affects the household. Your puppy will chew anything he can reach, chase your shoelaces, and play "tear the rag" with any piece of clothing he can find.

When puppies are newly born, they have no teeth. At about four weeks of age, puppies of most breeds begin to develop their deciduous (baby) teeth. They begin eating semi-solid food, biting and fighting with their littermates, and learning discipline from their mother. As their new teeth come in, they inflict pain on their mother's breasts, so feeding sessions become less frequent and shorter in duration. By six or eight weeks, the mother will start growling to warn her pups when they are fighting too roughly or hurting her as they nurse too much with their new teeth.

Puppies who play with chew toys will exhibit less destructive behavior and develop more physically.

CHEWING

Puppies need to chew, as it is a necessary part of their physical and mental development. They develop muscles and necessary life skills as they drag objects around, fight over possessions, and vocalize alerts and warnings. Puppies chew on things to explore their world. They are using their sense of taste to determine what is food and what is not. How else can they tell an electrical cord from a lizard?

At about four months of age, most puppies begin shedding their baby teeth. Often, these teeth need some help to come out to make way for the permanent teeth. The incisors (front teeth) will be replaced first. Then, the adult canine or fang teeth erupt. When a baby tooth is not shed before the permanent tooth comes in, veterinarians call it a retained deciduous tooth. This condition will often cause gum infections by trapping hair and debris between the permanent tooth and the retained baby tooth. Puppies who are given adequate chew toys will exhibit less destructive behavior, develop more physically, and have less chance of retained deciduous teeth.

VISITING THE VET

During the first year, your veterinarian should see your dog at regular intervals. Your vet will let you know when to bring your puppy in for vaccinations and parasite examinations. At each visit, your vet should inspect the lips, teeth, and mouth as part of a complete physical examination.

You should also take some part in the maintenance of your dog's oral health. Examine your dog's mouth weekly throughout his first year to make sure there are no sores, foreign objects, tooth problems, etc. If your dog drools excessively, shakes his head, or has bad breath, consult your veterinarian. By the time your dog is six months old, his permanent teeth are all in, and plaque can start to accumulate on the tooth surfaces. This is when your dog needs good dental-care habits to prevent buildup on his teeth.

Brushing is best—that is a fact that cannot be denied. However, some dogs do not like their teeth brushed regularly, or you may not be able to accomplish the task. In this case, you should consider a product that will help prevent plaque buildup, such as a Nylabone®.

Chewing will help your Yorkie shed his baby teeth to make room for his permanent teeth.

Yearly dental examinations performed by your veterinarian are critical to maintaining your Yorkshire Terrier's oral health.

PERIODONTAL DISEASE

By the time dogs are four years old, 75 percent of them have some type of periodontal disease; it is the most common infection in dogs. Yearly examinations by your vet are essential to maintaining your dog's good health. If periodontal disease is detected, he or she may recommend a prophylactic cleaning. To do a thorough cleaning, it will be necessary to put your dog under anesthesia.

With modern gas anesthetics and monitoring equipment, the procedure is fairly safe. Your veterinarian will scale the teeth with an ultrasound scaler or hand instrument. This removes the calculus from the teeth. If there are calculus deposits below the gum line, the veterinarian will plane the roots to make them smooth. After all of the calculus has been removed, the teeth are polished with pumice in a polishing cup. If any medical or surgical treatment is needed, it is done at this time. The final step would be fluoride treatment and your follow-up treatment at home. If the periodontal disease is advanced, the veterinarian may prescribe a medicated mouth rinse or antibiotics for use at home. Make sure your dog has safe, clean, and attractive chew toys, like Nylabones®, and healthy treats.

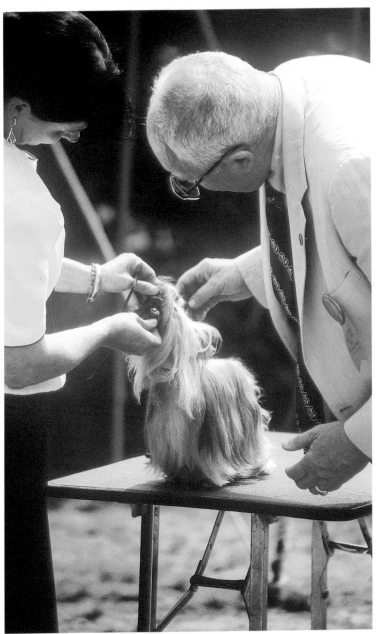

A Yorkshire Terrier gets his mouth and teeth examined at a show. It is important to remember, though, that dental health is essential for all dogs, not just show dogs.

MAINTAINING ORAL HEALTH

As your dog ages, professional examinations and cleanings should become more frequent. The mouth should be inspected at least once a year. Your vet may recommend visits every six months. In the geriatric patient, organs such as the heart, liver, and kidneys do not function as well as when your dog was young. Your vet will probably want to test these organs' functions prior to using general anesthesia for dental cleaning.

If your dog is a good chewer and you work closely with your vet, he can keep all of his teeth all of his life. However, as your dog ages, his sense of smell, sight, and taste will diminish. He may not have the desire to chase, trap, or chew his toys. He also will not have the energy to chew for long periods, as arthritis and periodontal disease could make chewing painful. This will leave you with more responsibility for keeping his teeth clean and healthy. However, the dog who would not let you brush his teeth at one year of age may let you brush his teeth now that he is ten years old.

If you train your dog with good chewing habits as a puppy, he will have healthier teeth throughout his life.

HEALTH CARE for Your Yorkshire Terrier

Yorkshire Terriers are very hardy little dogs, and they are generally quite healthy. A yearly trip to the veterinarian for an examination and vaccinations is all most Yorkies require. Medical emergencies, however, require immediate attention. These include severe burns or bleeding, unconsciousness, seizures, and unusually high or low temperatures. A few words here about vomiting and/or diarrhea—a toy dog can become dehydrated very quickly, and waiting until morning to take him to the veterinarian could make the difference between life and death.

Fortunately, veterinary medicine has become far more sophisticated than what it was in the past. This can be attributed to the increase in household pets, and consequently, the demand for better care for them. Also, human medicine has become far more complex. Today, diagnostic testing in veterinary medicine parallels human diagnostics. Because of better technology, we can expect our pets to live healthier lives, thereby increasing their life spans.

PHYSICAL EXAMS

During a physical exam, your veterinarian will check your pet's overall condition, which includes listening to the heart; checking the respiration; feeling the abdomen, muscles, and joints; checking the mouth, which includes looking at gum color and checking for signs of gum disease, along with plaque buildup; checking the ears for signs of an infection or ear mites; examining the eyes; and last but not least, checking the condition of the skin and coat.

The veterinarian should ask you questions regarding your pet's eating and elimination habits and invite you to relay your questions. It is a good idea to prepare a list so as not to forget anything. He or she should discuss the proper diet and the quantity to feed your pet. If this differs from your breeder's recommendation, you should convey to him or her what the breeder's choice is and see if he or she approves. If he or she recommends changing the diet, this should be done over a few days so as not to cause your dog gastrointestinal upset.

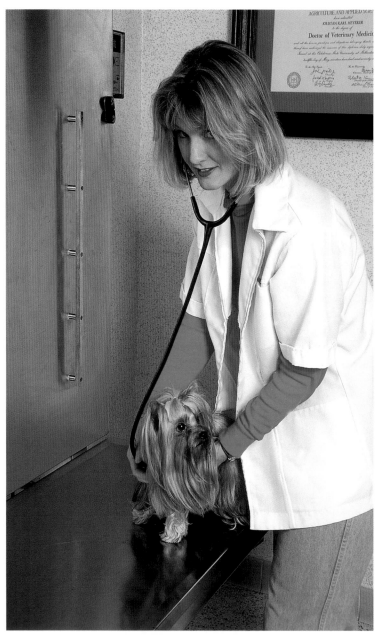

During a physical exam, your veterinarian will check your Yorkie's overall condition, including listening to the heart and checking respiration.

It is customary to take in a fresh stool sample (just a small amount) to test for intestinal parasites. It must be fresh, preferably within 12 hours, because the eggs hatch quickly and after hatching will not be able to be observed under the microscope. If your pet isn't obliging, the technician can usually take a sample in the clinic.

The First Checkup

You will want to take your new puppy/dog in for his first checkup within 48 to 72 hours after acquiring him. Many breeders strongly recommend this checkup, as do humane shelters. A puppy/dog can appear healthy, but he may have a serious problem that is not apparent to the layman. Most pets have some type of minor flaw that may never cause a real problem.

This first checkup is a good time to establish a relationship with your veterinarian and to learn the office policy regarding its hours and how the staff handles emergencies. Usually, the breeder or another conscientious pet owner is a good reference for locating a capable veterinarian. You should be aware that not all vets give the same quality of service. You should not make your selection based on the least expensive clinic, as you may be shortchanging your pet. There is also the possibility that the least expensive clinic might eventually cost you more due to improper diagnosis, treatment, etc.

If you are selecting a new veterinarian, feel free to ask for a tour of the clinic. You should inquire about making an appointment for a tour, because all clinics are working clinics and may not be available all day for sightseers. You may worry less if you see where your pet will be spending the day if he ever needs to be hospitalized.

Immunizations

It is important that you take your puppy/dog's vaccination record with you on your first visit. In the case of a puppy, presumably the breeder has seen to the vaccinations up to the time you acquired your pet. Veterinarians differ in their vaccination protocol. It is not unusual for your puppy to have received vaccinations for distemper, hepatitis, leptospirosis, parvovirus, and parainfluenza every two to three weeks from the age of five or six weeks. Usually, this is a combined injection and is typically called the DHLPP.

The DHLPP is given through at least 12 to 14 weeks of age, and it is customary to continue with another parvovirus vaccine at 16

Your Yorkshire Terrier must be properly vaccinated before being socialized with other dogs.

to 18 weeks. You may wonder why so many immunizations are necessary. A puppy inherits antibodies in the womb from his mother, but no one knows for sure when these antibodies actually leave the puppy's body, although it is customarily accepted that distemper antibodies are gone by 12 weeks. Usually, parvovirus antibodies are gone by 16 to 18 weeks of age. However, it is possible for the maternal antibodies to be gone much earlier or even at a later age. Therefore, immunizations are started at an early age. The vaccine will not give immunity, though, as long as maternal antibodies are present.

The rabies vaccination is given at three or six months of age, depending on your local laws. A vaccine for bordetella (kennel cough) is advisable and can be given any time from the age of five weeks. The coronavirus is not commonly given unless there is a problem locally. The Lyme vaccine is necessary in endemic areas. Lyme disease has been reported in 47 states.

After your puppy has completed his puppy vaccinations, you will continue to booster the DHLPP once a year. It is customary to booster the rabies one year after the first vaccine, and then, depending on where you live, the booster should be given every year or every three years, depending on your local laws. The Lyme and corona vaccines are boostered annually, and it is recommended that the bordetella be boostered every six to eight months.

Annual Visit

The annual checkup, which includes booster vaccinations, a check for intestinal parasites, and a test for heartworm, is extremely important. However, make sure to get this checkup from a qualified

A thorough annual physical examination is a necessary part of maintaining your Yorkshire Terrier's good health.

veterinarian, because more harm than good can come to your dog through improper vaccinations, possibly from inferior vaccines and/or the wrong schedule. It is also important for your veterinarian to know your dog, and this is especially true during middle age and through the geriatric years. Your older dog may require more than one physical a year. The annual physical is good preventive medicine. Through early diagnosis and subsequent treatment, your dog can maintain a longer and better quality of life.

COMMON CANINE DISEASES

Distemper
Distemper is virtually an incurable disease. If the dog recovers, he is subject to severe nervous disorders. The virus attacks every tissue in the body and resembles a bad cold with a fever. It can cause a runny nose and eyes and gastrointestinal disorders, which may lead to a poor appetite, vomiting, and diarrhea. Raccoons, foxes, wolves, mink, and other dogs carry the virus. Unvaccinated youngsters and senior citizens are very susceptible. This is still a common disease.

Hepatitis
Hepatitis is a virus that is most serious in very young dogs. It is spread by contact with an infected animal or its stool or urine. The virus affects the liver and kidneys and is characterized by high fever, depression, and lack of appetite. Recovered animals may be afflicted with chronic illnesses.

Leptospirosis
Leptospirosis is a bacterial disease transmitted by contact with the urine of infected dogs, rats, or other wildlife. It produces severe symptoms of fever, depression, jaundice, and internal bleeding and was fatal before the vaccine was developed. Recovered dogs can be carriers, and the disease can be transmitted from dogs to humans.

Parvovirus
Parvovirus was first noted in the late 1970s and is still a fatal disease. However, with proper vaccinations, early diagnosis, and prompt treatment, it is a manageable disease. It attacks the bone marrow and intestinal tract. Symptoms include depression, loss of

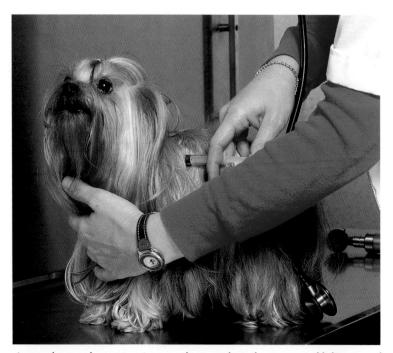

As your dog ages, he may require more than one physical per year; establishing a good relationship with your veterinarian is a must.

appetite, vomiting, diarrhea, and collapse. Immediate medical attention is necessary in order to manage the disease.

Rabies

Rabies is shed in the saliva and is carried by raccoons, skunks, foxes, other dogs, and cats. It attacks nerve tissue, resulting in paralysis and death. Rabies can be transmitted to people and is virtually always fatal. This disease is reappearing in the suburbs.

Bordetella (Kennel Cough)

The symptoms of bordetella are coughing, sneezing, hacking, and retching, accompanied by a nasal discharge usually lasting from a few days to several weeks. There are several disease-producing organisms responsible for this disease. The present vaccines are helpful but do not protect for all of the strains. It is usually not life threatening, but in some instances it can progress to a serious bronchopneumonia. The disease is highly contagious. The

Your veterinarian will vaccinate your Yorkie and/or administer oral preventives to guard against various canine diseases.

vaccination should be given routinely to dogs who come into contact with other dogs through boarding kennels, training classes, or visits to the groomer.

Coronavirus

Coronavirus is usually self-limiting and is not a life-threatening disease. It was first noted in the late 1970s, about a year before parvovirus. The virus produces a yellow/brown stool, and there may be depression, vomiting, and diarrhea.

Lyme Disease

Lyme disease was first diagnosed in the US in 1976 in Lyme, Connecticut, in people who lived in close proximity to the deer tick. The disease is usually spread by these ticks, and symptoms may include acute lameness, fever, swelling of joints, and loss of appetite. Your veterinarian can advise you if you live in an endemic area.

INTESTINAL PARASITES

Intestinal parasites are more prevalent in some areas than others. Climate, soil, and contamination are big factors contributing to the incidence of intestinal parasites. Eggs are passed in the stool, lie on the ground, and then become infective in a certain number of days. Each of the worms described below has a different life cycle. Your dog's best chance of becoming and remaining worm-free is to always keep your yard clean and free of the dog's fecal matter. A fenced-in yard keeps stray dogs out, which is certainly helpful.

Having a fecal examination performed on your dog twice a year, or more often if there is a problem, is recommended. If your dog has a positive fecal sample, he will be given the appropriate medication, and you will be asked to bring back another stool sample after a certain period of time (depending on the type of worm); then he will be rewormed. This process continues until he has at least two negative samples. Different types of worms require different medications. You will be wasting your money and doing your dog an injustice by buying over-the-counter medications without first consulting your veterinarian.

Hookworms

Hookworms are almost microscopic intestinal worms that can cause anemia and may lead to some serious problems, including death, in young puppies. Hookworms can be transmitted to humans through penetration of the skin. Puppies may be born with them.

Roundworms

Roundworms are spaghetti-like worms that can cause a potbellied appearance and dull coat, along with more severe symptoms such as vomiting, diarrhea, and coughing. Puppies acquire these while in the mother's uterus and through lactation. Both hookworms and roundworms may be acquired through ingestion.

Whipworms

Whipworms have a three-month life cycle and are not acquired through the dam. They cause intermittent diarrhea, usually with mucus. Whipworms are possibly the most difficult worm to eradicate. Their eggs are very resistant to most environmental factors and can last for years until the proper conditions enable them to mature. Whipworms are seldom seen in the stool.

OTHER INTERNAL PARASITES

Coccidiosis and Giardiasis

Coccidiosis and giardiasis, both protozoal infections, usually affect pups, especially in places where large numbers of puppies are brought together. Older dogs may harbor these infections but do not show signs unless they are stressed. Symptoms include diarrhea, weight loss, and lack of appetite. These infections are not always apparent in fecal examination.

Tapeworms

Seldom apparent on fecal floatation, tapeworms frequently show up as rice-like segments around the dog's anus and the base of the tail. Tapeworms are long, flat, and ribbon-like, sometimes several feet in length, and made up of many segments about $5/8$ of an inch long.

There are two common causes of tapeworm found in dogs. First, the larval form of the flea tapeworm parasite could mature in an intermediate host, the flea, before it can become infective. Your dog may acquire this by ingesting the flea through licking and chewing. Secondly, rabbits, rodents, and certain large game animals serve as

Although maternal antibodies temporarily protect puppies from disease, vaccinations are necessary to continue protection once the antibodies are no longer effective.

intermediate hosts for other species of tapeworms. If your dog eats one of these infected hosts, he can acquire tapeworms.

Heartworms

Heartworms are worms that reside in the heart and adjacent blood vessels of the lung. They produce microfilaria, which circulate in the bloodstream. It is possible for a dog to be infected with any number of these worms, which are 6 to 14 inches long. Heartworm disease is life-threatening and expensive to treat, but it is easily prevented. Depending on where you live, your veterinarian may recommend a preventive year-round and either an annual or semiannual blood test. The most common preventive is given once a month.

EXTERNAL PARASITES

Fleas

Fleas are not only a dog's worst enemies, but they are also enemies of the owner's pocketbook. The majority of dogs are allergic to the bite of a flea, and in many cases, it only takes one fleabite to require treatment. The protein in a flea's saliva is the culprit. Allergic dogs have a reaction, which usually results in a "hot spot." More than likely, such a reaction will involve a trip to the veterinarian for treatment. Fortunately, today there are several good products available to help prevent fleas and eliminate them when there is an outbreak.

If there is a flea infestation, no one product is going to correct the problem. Not only will the dog require treatment, but so will the environment. In general, flea collars are not always very effective, although there is an "egg" collar now available that will kill the eggs on the dog. Dips are the most economical, but they are messy. There are some effective shampoos and treatments available through pet shops and veterinarians.

Another popular parasiticide is permethrin, which is applied to the back of the dog in one or two places, depending on the dog's weight. This product works as a repellent, causing the flea to get "hot feet" and jump off. Do not confuse this product with some of the organophosphates that are also applied to the dog's back.

Some products are not usable on young puppies, and treating fleas should be done under your veterinarian's guidance. Frequently,

Although most dogs are allergic to fleabites, there are several products available that can alleviate the problem.

it is necessary to combine products, and the layman does not have enough knowledge regarding possible toxicities. It is hard to believe, but there are a few dogs who do have a natural resistance to fleas. Nevertheless, it would be wise to treat all pets at the same time. Don't forget your cats, either; cats just love to prowl the neighborhood and return with unwanted guests.

Adult fleas live on the dog, but their eggs drop off into the environment. There, they go through four larval stages before reaching adulthood, when they are able to jump back on the poor unsuspecting dog. The cycle resumes and takes between 21 to 28 days under ideal conditions. There are environmental products available that will kill both adult fleas and larvae.

Ticks

Ticks can carry Rocky Mountain Spotted Fever, Lyme disease, and can cause tick paralysis. They should be removed with tweezers. Try to pull out the head because the jaws carry disease. Tick preventive collars do an excellent job. Ticks automatically back out on those dogs wearing collars.

Sarcoptic Mange

The mite characterized by sarcoptic mange is difficult to find on skin scrapings. The female mite burrows under the skin and lays her eggs, which hatch within a few days. Sarcoptic mange causes intense itching in dogs and may even be characterized by hair loss in its early stages. Sarcoptes are highly contagious to other dogs and to humans, although they do not live long on humans.

Demodectic Mange

Demodectic mange is a mite that is passed from the dam to her puppies. It commonly affects youngsters aged three to ten months. Diagnosis is confirmed by skin scraping. Small areas of alopecia around the eyes, lips, and/or forelegs become visible. There is little itching unless there is a secondary bacterial infection. Some breeds are afflicted more than others.

Cheyletiella

Cheyletiella causes intense itching and is diagnosed by skin scraping. It lives in the outer layers of the skin of dogs, cats, rabbits,

Yorkshire Terriers should be examined frequently for signs of fleas, ticks, and other parasites, especially if they've been playing outside.

and humans. Yellow-gray scales may be found on the back and the rump, top of the head, and the nose.

OTHER MEDICAL PROBLEMS

Anal Sac Impaction/Inflammation

Anal sacs are small sacs on either side of the rectum that can cause the dog discomfort when they are full. They should empty when the dog has a bowel movement. Symptoms of inflammation or impaction include excessive licking under the tail and/or a bloody or sticky discharge from the anal area. Breeders recommend emptying the sacs on a regular schedule when bathing the dog. Many veterinarians, on the other hand, prefer that this not be done unless there are symptoms.

You can express the sacs by squeezing them (at the five and seven o'clock positions) in and up toward the anus. Take precautions not to get in the way of the foul-smelling fluid that is expressed. Some dogs object to this procedure, so it would be wise to have someone hold your dog's head at this time. Sometimes you will see your dog scooting his rear end along the floor, which is caused by anal-sac irritation and not worms.

Colitis

When the stool is blood or blood tinged, it could be the result of inflammation of the colon. Colitis, sometimes intermittent, can be the result of stress, undiagnosed whipworms, or perhaps may be idiopathic (no explainable reason for the condition). If intermittent bloody stools are an ongoing problem, you should probably feed a diet higher in fiber. Seek professional help if your dog seems to be suffering and/or the condition persists.

Conjunctivitis

Many breeds are prone to conjunctivitis. The conjunctiva is the pink tissue that lines the inner surface of the eyeball, with the exception of the clear, transparent cornea. Irritating substances such as bacteria, foreign matter, or chemicals can cause it to become reddened and swollen. It is important to keep any hair trimmed from around the eyes. Long hair stays damp and aggravates the problem. Keep the eyes cleaned with warm water, and wipe away any matter that has accumulated in the corner of the eyes. If the condition persists, you should see your veterinarian. This problem goes hand in hand with keratoconjunctivitis sicca.

Ear Infection

Otitis externa is an inflammation of the external ear canal that begins at the outside opening of the ear and extends inward to the eardrum. Dogs with pendulous ears are prone to this disease, but breeds with upright ears also have a high incidence of problems. Allergies, food, and inhalants, along with hormonal problems, such as hypothyroidism, are major contributors to the disease. For those dogs who have recurring problems, you need to investigate the underlying causes if you hope to cure them.

Be careful never to get water in the ears. Water provides a great medium for bacteria to grow. If your dog swims or you inadvertently get water in his ears, use a drying agent. You can use an at-home preparation of equal parts of 3-percent hydrogen peroxide and 70-percent rubbing alcohol. Another preparation is equal parts of white vinegar and water. As an alternative, your veterinarian can provide a suitable product. When cleaning the ears, use cotton-tip applicators extremely carefully, because they make it easy to pack debris down into the canal. Only clean what you can see.

If your dog has an ongoing infection, don't be surprised if your veterinarian recommends sedating him and flushing his ears with a bulb syringe. Sometimes this needs to be done a few times to get the ear clean. The ear must be clean so that medication can come into contact with the canal. Be prepared to return for checkups until the infection is gone. This may involve more flushing if the ears are badly infected.

For chronic or recurring cases, your veterinarian may recommend thyroid testing, etc., as well as a hypoallergenic diet for a trial period of 10 to 12 weeks. Depending on your dog, it may be a good idea to see a dermatologist. Ears shouldn't be taken lightly, because if the condition gets out of hand, surgery may be necessary. Ask your veterinarian to explain proper ear maintenance for your dog.

Fleabite Allergy

Fleabite allergy is the result of a hypersensitivity to the bite of a flea and its saliva. It only takes one bite to cause the dog to chew or scratch himself raw. Your dog may need medical attention to ease his discomfort. You should clip the hair around the "hot spot" and

Good breeders make every effort to plan each breeding cycle with regard to conformation, temperament, and health.

wash it with mild soap and water, and you may need to do this daily if the area weeps. Apply an antibiotic anti-inflammatory product. Hot spots can occur from other trauma as well, such as grooming.

Interdigital Cysts

Check for interdigital cysts on your dog's feet if he shows signs of lameness. They are frequently associated with staph infections and can be quite painful. A home remedy is to soak the infected foot in a solution of 1/2 teaspoon of bleach in a couple of quarts of water. Do this two to three times a day for a couple of days. Check with your veterinarian for an alternative remedy; antibiotics usually work well. If there is a recurring problem, surgery may be required.

Lameness

Lameness may be caused by an interdigital cyst, or it could be caused by a mat between the toes, especially if your dog licks his feet. Sometimes it is hard to determine which leg is affected. If your dog is holding up his leg, you need to see your veterinarian.

Poor Skin

Frequently, poor skin is the result of an allergy to fleas, inhalants, or food. These types of problems usually result in a staph dermatitis. Dogs with food allergies usually show signs of severe itching and scratching, though some dogs with food allergies never itch. Their only symptom is a swelling of the ears with no ear infection. Food allergy may result in recurrent bacterial skin and ear infections. Your veterinarian or dermatologist will recommend a good restricted diet.

Inhalant allergies result in atopy, which causes licking of the feet, scratching of the body, and rubbing of the muzzle. These allergies may be seasonable. Your veterinarian or dermatologist can perform intradermal testing for inhalant allergies. If your dog should test positive, then a vaccine may be prepared.

Tonsillitis

Usually, young dogs have a higher incidence of tonsillitis than older dogs because older dogs have a built-up resistance. It is very contagious. Sometimes it is difficult to determine if the condition is tonsillitis or kennel cough because the symptoms are similar. Symptoms of tonsillitis include fever, poor eating, difficulty swallowing, and retching up a white, frothy mucus.

Spaying and Neutering

More than likely, your breeder has requested that you have your puppy neutered or spayed. Your breeder's request is based on what is healthiest for your dog and what is most beneficial for your breed. Experienced and conscientious breeders devote many years to developing a bloodline. In order to do this, they make every effort to plan each breeding cycle with regard to conformation, temperament, and health.

A responsible breeder does his or her best to perform the necessary testing (i.e. OFA, CERF, testing for inherited blood disorders, thyroid, etc.). Testing is expensive and sometimes very disheartening when a favorite dog doesn't pass his health tests. The health history pertains not only to the breeding stock but also to the immediate ancestors.

Reputable breeders do not want their offspring to be bred indiscriminately. Therefore, you may be asked to neuter or spay your puppy. Of course, there is always the exception, and the breeder may agree to let you breed your dog under his or her direct supervision. This is an important concept. More and more effort is being made to breed healthier dogs.

Your Yorkshire Terrier's breeder may request that you have the puppy spayed or neutered.

The Benefits of Spaying and Neutering

As mentioned earlier, there are numerous benefits to spaying or neutering your dog. Intact males and females may be prone to housetraining accidents. Females urinate frequently before, during, and after heat cycles, and males tend to mark territory if there is a female in heat. Males may show the same behavior if there are guests or a visiting dog. Spaying and neutering may virtually eliminate these behaviors.

Surgery involves a sterile operating procedure equivalent to human surgery. The incision site is shaved, surgically scrubbed, and draped. The veterinarian wears a sterile surgical gown, cap, mask, and gloves. It is customary for the veterinarian to recommend a pre-anesthetic blood screening, looking for metabolic problems, and an ECG rhythm strip to check for normal heart function. Today, anesthetics are equal to human anesthetics, which means your dog can walk out of the clinic the same day as surgery.

Spaying

Unspayed females are subject to mammary and ovarian cancer. In order to prevent mammary cancer, a female must be spayed prior to her first heat cycle. Later in life, an unspayed female may develop a pyometra (an infected uterus), a life-threatening condition.

Spaying is performed at about six months of age under a general anesthetic and is easy on the young dog. As you might expect, it is a little harder on the older dog, but that is no reason to deny her the surgery. The surgery removes the ovaries and uterus. It is important to remove all of the ovarian tissue. If some is left behind, she could remain attractive to males. In order to view the ovaries, a reasonably long incision is necessary. An ovariohysterectomy is considered major surgery.

Neutering

Neutering the male at a young age will inhibit some characteristic male behavior that owners frown upon. Some males will not hike their legs and mark territory if they are neutered at six months of age. Also, neutering at a young age has hormonal benefits, lessening the chance of hormonal aggressiveness.

Surgery involves removing the testicles but leaving the scrotum. If there should be a retained testicle, the male definitely needs to be neutered before the age of two or three years, because retained

While some people worry about their dogs gaining weight after being spayed or neutered, this doesn't usually occur, especially if they receive a sufficient amount of exercise.

testicles can develop cancer. Unneutered males are at risk for testicular cancer, perineal fistulas, perianal tumors and fistulas, and prostatic disease.

After the Surgery

Some people worry about their dogs gaining weight after being neutered or spayed. This is usually not the case. It is true that some dogs may be less active, so they could develop a problem, but most are just as active as they were before surgery. However, if your dog should begin to gain weight, you need to decrease his or her food and see to it that he or she gets a little more exercise.

BREEDING Your Yorkshire Terrier

MAKING THE DECISION

There are many good books available on genetics and breeding. Should you decide to breed your bitch, do your homework first. Breeding a toy dog is not without risk. Please study your standard first. Is your dog of good enough quality to breed? Are you willing to take the risk? If everything goes well, you may have a rewarding experience. But if it doesn't, and sometimes all doesn't go well, can you take the heartache? You probably won't make a profit. Can you afford some very costly veterinary bills should complications arise? Do you have the time? There will be a trip for the mating and many watchful hours spent before, during, and after the delivery. The puppies will weigh from 2 to 6 ounces at birth. Their first few days are very critical and require constant monitoring. If puppies require

Your new Yorkshire Terrier puppies will need a good veterinarian who has experience with toy dogs.

Breeding your Yorkshire Terrier will require a great deal of time, dedication, and expense.

hand-raising or supplemental feeding, you may be feeding them every two to three hours around the clock! Young weanling puppies chew up everything and seem to eliminate much more than they eat! Is breeding restricted in your area? Check the rules, because you might be breaking the law! In some areas "lemon laws" are now in existence, and you will have to guarantee the puppies by replacement or possibly costs and refunds.

If you still want to try it, is your bitch of quality to breed? I have a rule that if the dog isn't of quality to show, she is not of quality to breed. Hopefully you have purchased your female from a reputable breeder. The earliest possible time she should be bred is at the age of 18 months, or at least the second heat. Ask the breeder to help you evaluate the bitch and decide if she is of quality to breed and to help you decide which sire you should select. No one knows what sire to try better than the breeder of the bitch. Your breeder knows the line of dogs and what they can produce. The breeder also knows whether you should breed in the line or outcross to another line. This has probably been tried with the same family of dogs, so why not take advantage of prior experience? We've all got to start somewhere, but take the advice of a mentor in the beginning. You'll want to try your own ideas later, but it is too overwhelming for the beginner to attempt alone.

Preparing to Breed

A good veterinarian is a must. Make sure he or she has experience with toy dogs. Take your bitch for a checkup before she is bred. Notify the veterinarian when the time is near for the whelping (usually 59 to 63 days after mating). Don't hesitate to get help if anything seems unusual. I don't believe in the theory "let nature take its course." We have developed these breeds of dogs for our own purpose in the world. A toy dog could not survive in the wild; we have taken nature into our own hands.

When your bitch first comes into season, notify the owner of the stud to make the arrangements. The stud fee is to be paid at the time of service, and a return service is usually guaranteed if there are no puppies. A toy dog owner will probably not give a puppy as part of the service fee as the litters are small, and the owner won't want to give up his only puppy. When the bleeding stops and the vulva begins to soften, usually at 10 or 11 days, the bitch is usually ready to be bred.

Pregnancy and Labor

The pregnancy will last nine weeks. Your bitch may go off her food or have a little morning sickness around three weeks. You usually cannot tell for sure that she is pregnant before the fourth or fifth week, at which time you may increase her food intake. If she becomes quite large, you may have to coax her to eat near the end of her pregnancy and feed her several small meals per day. When the time comes to whelp, she may refuse to eat or drink. A dog's temperature is normally 101°F. Begin checking the temperature about one week before the puppies are due. When the temperature drops below 99°F, the puppies will usually be born within 24 hours.

In the first stages of labor, the bitch will seem uncomfortable. She may dig or nest frantically. All types of whelping boxes may be made or purchased, but a cardboard box cut down makes a great whelping box. Put the bitch in a dog pen with her box. This will be her home with her babies. She will urinate and defecate often during this early stage of labor while the cervix is dilating. Next, you will usually see a dark water sack appear.

Keeping the new puppies warm is critical to their survival; the temperature in the whelping box should be between 85°F to 90°F.

101

THE BIRTH

The puppy should be born within an hour after you see the water sack. You may touch the sack with a clean hand to see if the puppy is there. As soon as the puppy starts to emerge, it needs to be born quickly. Try to let the bitch do it on her own, but if she has difficulty or if you see the puppy's feet or buttocks, you may have to help her. Take a washcloth and grasp the puppy. Pull gently but firmly in a downward motion along with the contractions. It will help here if you have a friend to hold the bitch. If it is her first puppy and it is stuck tight, your little "sweetie" may try to bite your hand off! Once she sees the baby, she will be pleased and will begin to lick it. Be sure to break the membranes from the puppy's face and clear the mouth. If the placenta does not come out with the puppy, you may put forceps about 1 inch out on the cord and another pair of forceps behind that one. Cut the cord between the forceps. When you release the hemostat (forceps) from the cord, you may need to tie it with dental floss if it bleeds. Hold the baby upside down to clear the throat. Rub him quite briskly to see that he is breathing. If he is not breathing, don't give up—just keep rubbing him and working with him, and he will usually begin to breathe. Now you may take the other forceps and gently pull the placenta from the bitch. If you should lose it, it will usually come out with the next puppy. If you don't think you have counted a placenta for each puppy, notify your veterinarian so he can give her a hormone injection as a clean-up shot.

Have a hot water bottle or heating pad to warm the babies. You may give the puppy to the bitch until the next one begins to arrive, and then you might want to remove the previously born puppy and put him on the heating pad to keep him warm.

A newborn puppy cannot regulate his body temperature until he is about 10 to 12 days old. It has been said that the number-one killer of newborns is chilling. The temperature in the box needs to be 85°F to 90°F. You may use a heat lamp or a heating pad on a low setting under the box rather than heat the whole room to that temperature. Mom may be a little warm, but this is usually more from her temperature rising from 99°F back up to 101°F and from the letdown of her milk. You will need to make sure that the bitch cleans the puppies' rear ends to clean the mecomium, or first stool, which is a dark substance from the intestinal tract. If she doesn't do a good job of this, use a warm, moist piece of cotton and massage the puppies' anuses.

Your Yorkshire Terrier puppies should be fed dry puppy food softened with water or canned milk at around three weeks of age.

All puppies need the colostrum, which is the mother's first milk. If they don't readily crawl to the nipples, help them by placing the nipples into their mouths. Some bitches will have a puppy every 15 to 30 minutes, but it can take several hours between puppies. If she seems very distressed or pushes for 30 minutes, call the veterinarian.

After she is finished whelping, she will usually curl around her babies for a rest. Take Mom and puppies to your veterinarian for a postnatal check.

AFTER THE BIRTH

Three to four days after their birth, you will need to take the puppies to the veterinarian to have their dewclaws removed and their tails docked. Some countries are now frowning upon the docking of tails. The Yorkshire Terrier Club of America has voted not to allow for long tails in the standard, which still says, "the tail is to be docked to mid-length." We find this procedure not to be that traumatic when done properly at a young age. The non-docked tail with long coat causes a Yorkshire to have a very dirty rear end. It also spoils the look of the dog.

Depending on their environment, puppies begin a series of vaccinations between five and eight weeks of age.

Begin to feed your puppies with a little dry puppy food softened with water or canned milk at around three weeks of age. I allow my puppies to remain with their mother until she is tired of them and they are eating well. Most Yorkshire puppies do not wean early. I feed the bitch all she wants when she is nursing puppies. She will usually enjoy cleaning up the puppies' food. Most of my females weigh more when the puppies are weaned than they did right after the puppies' birth. Feed your puppies three or four times a day, and don't leave old food in their pen because they don't like it after it sits there for an hour. I usually leave a bowl of very small dry kibbles in the pen in case one of them needs a snack. Make certain all the puppies are eating! A little puppy can become hypoglycemic and even die if he forgets to eat. At the first sign of loose stool, take a sample to the veterinarian to make sure there are no parasites.

Puppies must begin a series of vaccinations between five and eight weeks old, depending on their environment. I start my puppies early, especially in the warm months when insects can carry

Perhaps the most important thing that a breeder can do is to meet prospective owners to ensure that the puppies will be loved and treated well in their new homes.

germs and when I am actively attending dog shows. Ask your veterinarian when to begin vaccinations, and set up a schedule for your puppies to receive the appropriate vaccinations at the appropriate times.

SELLING THE PUPPIES

I never sell Yorkshire puppies before they are 12 weeks old. At this age, I can evaluate the puppies for show potential. They have also had several vaccinations and are eating well.

Be very careful where you sell your puppies. Interview the prospective buyers to make certain they will treat the puppy well and provide the same care and love you have provided. Sell all of your puppies that are not of show potential with a limited registration and/or neutering agreement. Guarantee the health of your puppies.

Be sure to have an agreement with the new owners that you will take the dog back if they can't keep him any longer. By doing this, you will always be sure your dogs are in suitable homes.

A diet and vaccination sheet should accompany the new puppy, along with a receipt, contract, and registration application. Please make sure the new owners have your telephone number and the number of your veterinarian.

SPORT of Purebred Dogs

Welcome to the exciting and sometimes frustrating sport of dogs. Dog showing has been a very popular sport for a long time and has been taken quite seriously by some, while others only enjoy it as a hobby. This section covers the basics that may entice you, further your knowledge, and help you to understand the dog world.

The Kennel Club in England was formed in 1859, the American Kennel Club was established in 1884, and the Canadian Kennel Club was formed in 1888. The purpose of these clubs was to register purebred dogs and maintain their studbooks. In the beginning, the concept of registering dogs was not readily accepted. However, more than 36 million dogs have been enrolled in the AKC Studbook since its inception in 1888. Presently, the kennel clubs not only register dogs, but they also adopt and enforce rules and regulations

Puppy kindergarten class is a great way for your Yorkie to socialize with other dogs, as well as learn some beginning obedience.

governing dog shows, obedience trials, and field trials. Over the years they have fostered and encouraged interest in the health and welfare of the purebred dog. They routinely donate funds to veterinary research for study on genetic disorders.

Today there are numerous activities that are enjoyable for both the dog and the handler. Some of the activities include conformation showing, obedience competition, tracking, agility, the Canine Good Citizen® Program, and a wide range of instinct tests that vary from breed to breed. Where you start depends upon your goals, which early on may not be readily apparent.

PUPPY KINDERGARTEN

Every puppy will benefit from this class. Puppy Kindergarten Training (PKT) is the foundation for all future dog activities, from conformation to "couch potatoes." Pet owners should make an effort to attend, even if they never expect to show their dogs. The class is designed for puppies about three months of age, with graduation at approximately five months of age. All of the puppies will be in the same age group, and even though some may be a little unruly, there should not be any real problem.

The class will teach the puppy some beginning obedience. As in all obedience classes, the owner will learn how to train his or her own dog. The PKT class gives the puppy the opportunity to interact with other puppies in the same age group and exposes him to strangers, which is very important. Without training, some dogs grow up and develop some problem behaviors, one of them being fear of strangers. As you can see, there can be much to gain from this class.

There are some basic obedience exercises that every dog should learn, and the foundations for some of these exercises may be learned in puppy kindergarten.

Sit

One way of teaching the sit is to use a treat, holding it over the dog's head. The dog will need to sit to get the treat, at which point you should tell him to sit, then praise him and give him the treat. If your dog does not automatically sit when you hold the treat over his head, pull up on the leash, and at the same time, reach around his hind legs with your left hand and tuck them in. As you are doing this, say the dog's name and then say, "Sit." Always use the dog's name when you give an active command.

One way of teaching your Yorkie to sit is by holding a small treat above his head so that he will have to sit to get the treat.

Encourage the dog to hold the sit for a few seconds, which will eventually be the beginning of the sit-stay. Depending on how cooperative he is, you can rub him under the chin or stroke his back. This is a good time to establish eye contact.

Down

Sit the dog on your left side, and kneel down beside him with the leash in your right hand. Reach over him with your left hand and grasp his left foreleg. With your right hand, take his right foreleg and pull his legs forward while you say, "Down." If he tries to get up, lean on his shoulder to encourage him to stay down. It will relax your dog if you stroke his back while he is down. Try to encourage him to stay down for a few seconds as preparation for the down-stay.

Heel

The definition of heeling is the dog walking under control at your left heel. Your puppy will learn controlled walking in his puppy kindergarten class, which will eventually lead to heeling. Give the command, saying his name and "heel," and start off briskly with your left foot. Your leash should be in your right hand, and your left hand should be holding it about halfway down. Your left hand should be able to control the leash, and there should be a little slack in it.

You want your dog to walk with you with your leg somewhere between his nose and his shoulder. You need to encourage him to stay with you and discourage him from forging ahead or lagging behind you. It is best to keep him on a fairly short lead. Do not allow the lead to become tight. It is far better to give him a little jerk when necessary and remind him to heel. When you come to a halt, be prepared to physically make him sit. It takes practice to become coordinated. There are excellent books on training that you may wish to purchase, and your instructor should be able to recommend one for you.

Recall

Recall is quite possibly the most important exercise you will ever teach. It should be a pleasant experience. The puppy may learn to do random recalls while being attached to a long line such as a clothesline. Later, the exercise will start with the dog sitting and staying until called.

Your Yorkshire Terrier should be introduced to the down-stay gradually, after he is comfortable with the down.

The command is the dog's name and then "come." Let your command be happy. You want your dog to come willingly and faithfully, because the recall could save his life if he sneaks out the door. In practicing the recall, let him jump on you or touch you before you reach for him. If he is shy, kneel down to his level. Reaching for an insecure dog could frighten him, and he may not be willing to come again in the future.

Lots of praise and a treat are in order whenever you do a recall. Under no circumstances should you ever correct your dog when he has come to you. Later, in formal obedience, your dog will be required to sit in front of you after recalling and then go to heel position.

Canine Good Citizen® Program

The AKC sponsors a program to encourage dog owners to train their dogs. Local clubs perform the pass/fail tests, and dogs that pass are awarded a Canine Good Citizen® Certificate. Proof of vaccination is required at the time of participation. The test includes:

1. Accepting a friendly stranger.
2. Sitting politely for petting.
3. Appearance and grooming.
4. Walking on a loose leash.
5. Walking through a crowd.
6. Sit and down on command/staying in place.
7. Coming when called.
8. Reaction to another dog.
9. Reactions to distractions.
10. Supervised separation.

CONFORMATION

Conformation showing is the oldest dog show sport. This type of showing is based on the dog's appearance—that is, his structure, movement, and attitude. When considering this type of showing, you need to be aware of your breed's standard and be able to

The Canine Good Citizen® Program, sponsored by the AKC, encourages dog owners to train their dogs.

evaluate your dog compared to that standard. The breeder of your puppy or other experienced breeders would be good sources for such an evaluation. Puppies can go through many changes over a period of time. Many puppies start out as promising hopefuls and then after maturing may be disappointing as show candidates. Even so, this should not deter them from being excellent pets.

Local kennel clubs or obedience clubs usually offer conformation training classes. These are excellent places for training puppies. The puppy should be able to walk on a lead before entering such a class. Proper ring procedure and technique for posing (stacking) the dog will be demonstrated, as well as gaiting the dog. Generally, certain patterns are used in the ring, such as the triangle or the "L." Conformation class, like the PKT class, will give your puppy the opportunity to socialize with different breeds of dog as well as humans.

It takes some time to learn the routine of conformation showing. Usually, one starts at the AKC-sanctioned puppy matches or fun matches. These matches are generally for puppies from 2 or 3 months to a year old, and there may be classes for the adult over the age of 12 months. Similar to point shows, the classes are divided by sex, and after completion of the classes in that breed or variety, the class winners compete for Best of Breed or Variety. The winner goes on to compete in the Group, and the Group winners compete for Best in Match. No championship points are awarded for match wins.

A few matches can be great training for puppies, even if you don't intend to go on showing. Matches enable the puppy to meet new people and be handled by a stranger—the judge. It also offers a change of environment, which broadens the horizon for both dog and handler. Matches and other dog activities boost the confidence of the handler, especially the younger handlers.

Conformation in the United States

The AKC championship is built on a point system, which is different from Great Britain. To become an AKC Champion of Record, the dog must earn 15 points. The number of points earned each time depends upon the number of dogs in competition. The number of points available at each show depends upon the breed, its sex, and the location of the show. The US is divided into ten AKC zones. Each zone has its own set of points. The purpose of the

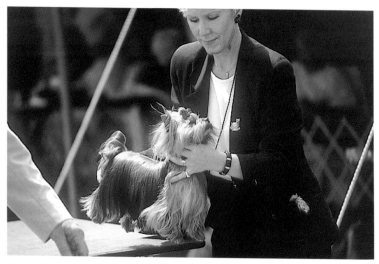

For toy dogs, part of conformation showing is learning to stand still on a table to be examined by the judges.

zones is to try to equalize the points available from breed to breed and area to area. The AKC adjusts the point scale annually.

The number of points that can be won at a show are between one and five. Three-, four- and five-point wins are considered majors. Not only does the dog need 15 points won under three different judges, but those points must include two majors under two different judges. Canada also works on a point system, but majors are not required.

Males always show before bitches. The classes available to those seeking points are: Puppy (which may be divided into 6 to 9 months and 9 to 12 months); 12 to 18 months; Novice; Bred-by-Exhibitor; American-bred; and Open. The class winners of the same sex of each breed or variety compete against each other for Winners Dog and Winners Bitch. A Reserve Winners Dog and Reserve Winners Bitch are also awarded but do not carry any points unless the original win is disallowed by the AKC. The Winners Dog and Bitch compete with the Specials (those dogs who have attained a championship) for Best of Breed or Variety, Best of Winners, and Best of Opposite Sex. It is possible to pick up an extra point or even a major if the points are higher for the defeated winner than those of Best of Winners. The latter would get the higher total from the defeated winner.

Author Janet Jackson shows one of her Yorkshire Terriers, Ch. Steppin' Up Cruella Deville.

A beautiful, well-groomed Yorkshire Terrier will make a distinct impression in the show ring.

At an all-breed show, each Best of Breed or Variety winner will go on to his respective Group, and then the Group winners will compete against each other for Best in Show. There are seven Groups: Sporting, Hounds, Working, Terriers, Toys, Non-Sporting, and Herding. Obviously, there are no Groups at specialty shows (those shows that have only one breed or a show such as the American Spaniel Club's Flushing Spaniel Show, which is for all flushing spaniel breeds).

Conformation in England

Earning a championship in England is somewhat different because England does not have a point system. Challenge Certificates are awarded if the judge feels the dog is deserving, regardless of the number of dogs in competition. A dog must earn three Challenge Certificates under three different judges, with at least one of these Certificates being won after the age of 12 months. Competition is very strong, and entries may be higher than they are in the US. The Kennel Club's Challenge Certificates are only available at championship shows.

In England, the Kennel Club regulations require that certain dogs, Border Collies and gundog breeds, qualify in a working capacity (i.e. obedience or field trials) before becoming a Full

It takes time to learn the routine of conformation showing, but AKC-sanctioned puppy matches or fun matches are a good place to start.

Champion. If they do not qualify in the working aspect, then they are designated a show champion, which is equivalent to the AKC's Champion of Record. A gundog may be granted the title of Field Trial Champion (FTCh.) if he passes all of the tests in the field, but he would also have to qualify in conformation before becoming a Full Champion. A Border Collie who earns the title of Obedience Champion (ObCh.) must also qualify in the conformation ring before becoming a champion.

The US doesn't have a designation for Full Champion but does award for Dual and Triple Champions. The Dual Champion must be a Champion of Record and either a Champion Tracker, Herding Champion, Obedience Trial Champion, or Field Champion. Any dog who has been awarded the titles of Champion of Record and any two of the following: Champion Tracker, Herding Champion, Obedience Trial Champion, or Field Champion, may be designated as a Triple Champion.

Showing in the United States and England

Conformation shows in England seem to put more emphasis on breeder judges than those in the US. There is much competition within the breeds. Therefore, the quality of the individual breeds should be very good. In the US, there tend to be more "all-around judges" (those who judge multiple breeds), with breeder judges used at the specialty shows. Breeder judges are more familiar with their own breed, as they are actively breeding that breed or did so at one time. Americans emphasize Group and Best in Show wins and promote them accordingly.

The shows in England can be very large and extend over several days, with the Groups scheduled on different days. Though multi-day shows are not common in the US, there are cluster shows in which several different clubs will use the same show site over consecutive days.

Westminster Kennel Club

The Westminster Kennel Club is the most prestigious dog show in the US, although the entry is limited to 2,500. In recent years, entry has been limited to champions. This show is more formal than the majority of the shows, with the judges wearing formal attire and the handlers fashionably dressed. In most instances, the quality of the dogs is superb— after all, it is a show of champions! It is a good show to study the AKC registered breeds and is by far

Ch. Steppin' Up Billy the Kid in the Westminster Kennel Club Group ring with his owner, author Janet Jackson.

the most exciting—especially because it is televised. Westminster is one of the few shows in this country that is still benched. This means the dog must be in his benched area during the show hours, except when he is being groomed, is in the ring, or is being exercised.

Typically, the handlers are very particular about their appearances. They are careful not to wear something that will detract from their dogs; instead, they try to wear clothing that will enhance their dogs. American ring procedure is quite formal compared to that of other countries. There is a certain etiquette expected between the judge and exhibitor and among the other exhibitors. Of course, it is not always the case, but the judge is supposed to be polite, not engaging in small talk or acknowledging how well he or she knows the handler. There is a more informal and relaxed atmosphere at the shows in other countries; for instance, the dress code is more casual. The US is very handler-oriented in many of the breeds.

Crufts

In England, Crufts is the Kennel Club's show and is most assuredly the largest dog show in the world. It's been known to have an entry of nearly 20,000, and the show lasts four days. Entry is only gained by qualifying through winning in specified classes at another championship show. Westminster is strictly conformation, but Crufts exhibitors and spectators enjoy not only conformation, but also obedience, agility, and a multitude of exhibitions as well. Obedience was admitted in 1957 and agility in 1983.

Junior Showmanship

The Junior Showmanship Class is a wonderful way to build self-confidence, even if there are no aspirations of staying with the dog showing later in life. Frequently, Junior Showmanship becomes the background of those who become successful exhibitors/handlers in the future. In some instances, it is taken very seriously, and success is measured in terms of wins. The Junior Handler is judged solely on his or her ability and skill in presenting his or her dog. The dog's conformation is not to be considered by the judge. Even so, the condition and grooming of the dog may be a reflection upon the handler.

Usually, the matches and point shows include different classes. The Junior Handler's dog may be entered in a breed or obedience class and even shown by another person in that class. Junior Showmanship classes are usually divided by age. The age is determined by the handler's age on the day of the show. The classes are:

Novice Junior for those at least 10 and under 14 years of age, who at the time of entry closing have not won three first places in a Novice Class at a licensed or member show.

Novice Senior for those at least 14 and under 18 years of age, who at the time of entry closing have not won three first places in a Novice Class at a licensed or member show.

Open Junior for those at least 10 and under 14 years of age, who at the time of entry closing have won at least three first places in a Novice Junior Showmanship Class at a licensed or member show with competition present.

Open Senior for those at least 14 and under 18 years of age, who at the time of entry closing have won at least three first places in a Novice Junior Showmanship Class at a licensed or member show with competition present.

Junior Handlers must include their AKC Junior Handler number on each show entry. This needs to be obtained from the AKC.

Apparel and Supplies

If you are handling your own dog, please give some consideration to your apparel. The dress code at matches is more informal than at the point shows. However, you should wear something a little more appropriate than beach attire or ragged jeans and bare feet. If you check out the handlers and see what is presently fashionable, you'll catch on. Men usually dress with a shirt and tie and a nice sports coat. Whether you are male or female, you will want to wear comfortable clothes and shoes. You need to be able to run with your dog, and you certainly don't want to take a chance of falling and hurting yourself. Women usually wear a dress or two-piece outfit, preferably with pockets to carry bait, brush, etc. The length of a woman's skirt or dress should be considered in case she needs to kneel on the floor, as should the ability of the dress or outfit to provide freedom of movement when running.

Professional but comfortable attire should be worn in the show ring when competing with your Yorkie.

You need to take along the following items to the show with your dog: crate; ex pen (if you use one); extra bedding; water pail and water; all required grooming equipment; table; chair for you; bait for dog and lunch for you and friends; and last but not least, clean-up materials, such as plastic bags, paper towels, and perhaps a damp towel—just in case. Don't forget your entry confirmation and directions to the show.

If you are showing in obedience, you may want to wear pants. Many top obedience handlers wear pants that are color-coordinated with their dogs. The philosophy is that imperfections in the black dog will be less obvious next to the handler's black pants.

Whether you are showing in conformation, Junior Showmanship, or obedience, you need to watch the clock and be sure you are not late. It is customary to pick up your conformation armband a few minutes before the start of the class. They will not wait for you, and if you are on the show grounds and not in the ring, you will upset everyone. It's a little more complicated picking up your obedience armband if you show later in the class. If you have not picked it up and they get to your number, you may not be allowed to show. It's best to pick up your armband early, but be aware that you may show earlier than expected if other handlers don't pick up. Customarily, all conflicts should be discussed with the judge prior to the start of the class.

OBEDIENCE

Obedience is necessary, without a doubt, but it can also become a wonderful hobby and even an obsession. Obedience classes and competition can provide wonderful companionship, not only with your dog but also with your classmates or fellow competitors. It is always gratifying to discuss your dog's problems with others who have had similar experiences. The AKC acknowledged obedience around 1936, and it has changed tremendously, even though many of the exercises are basically the same. Today, obedience competition is just that—very competitive. Even so, it is possible for every obedience exhibitor to come home a winner (by earning qualifying scores), even though he or she may not earn a placement in the class.

Most of the obedience titles are awarded after earning three qualifying scores (legs) in the appropriate class under three different judges. These classes offer a perfect score of 200, which is extremely rare. Each of the class exercises has its own point value. A leg is earned after receiving a score of at least 170 and at least 50 percent of the points available in each exercise. The titles are:

Companion Dog—CD

This is called the Novice Class, and the exercises are:

1.	Heel on leash and figure 8	40 points
2.	Stand for examination	30 points
3.	Heel free	40 points
4.	Recall	30 points
5.	Long sit—one minute	30 points
6.	Long down—three minutes	30 points
	Maximum total score	200 points

Companion Dog Excellent—CDX

This is the Open Class, and the exercises are:

1.	Heel off leash and figure 8	40 points
2.	Drop on recall	30 points
3.	Retrieve on flat	20 points
4.	Retrieve over high jump	30 points
5.	Broad jump	20 points
6.	Long sit—three minutes (out of sight)	30 points
7.	Long down—five minutes (out of sight)	30 points
	Maximum total score	200 points

Utility Dog—UD

The Utility Class exercises are:

1.	Signal exercise	40 points
2.	Scent discrimination-Article 1	30 points
3.	Scent discrimination-Article 2	30 points
4.	Directed retrieve	30 points
5.	Moving stand and examination	30 points
6.	Directed jumping	40 points
	Maximum total score	200 points

After achieving the UD title, you may feel inclined to go after the UDX and/or OTCh. The UDX (Utility Dog Excellent) title went into effect in January 1994. It is not easily attained. The title requires qualifying simultaneously ten times in Open B and Utility B, but not necessarily at consecutive shows.

The OTCh. (Obedience Trial Champion) is awarded after the dog has earned his UD and then goes on to earn 100 championship points, a first place in Utility, a first place in Open, and another first place in either class. The placements must be won under three different judges at all-breed obedience trials. The points are determined by the number of dogs competing in the Open B and Utility B classes. The OTCh. title precedes the dog's name.

Obedience matches (AKC-sanctioned, fun, and show-and-go) are often available. Usually, they are sponsored by the local obedience clubs. When preparing an obedience dog for a title, you will find matches very helpful. Fun matches and show-and-go matches are more lenient in allowing you to make corrections in the ring. This type of training is usually very necessary for the Open and

Utility classes. AKC-sanctioned obedience matches do not allow corrections in the ring because they must abide by the AKC obedience regulations booklet. If you are interested in showing in obedience, you should contact the AKC for a copy of *Obedience Regulations.*

TRACKING

Tracking is officially classified as obedience. There are three tracking titles available: Tracking Dog (TD), Tracking Dog Excellent (TDX), and Variable Surface Tracking (VST). If all three tracking titles are obtained, then the dog officially becomes a CT (Champion Tracker). The CT will go in front of the dog's name.

A TD may be earned anytime and does not have to follow the other obedience titles. There are many exhibitors who prefer tracking to obedience, and there are others who do both.

Tracking Dog—TD

A dog must be certified by an AKC tracking judge to perform in an AKC test. The AKC can provide the names of tracking judges in your area that you can contact for certification. Depending on where you live, you may have to travel a distance if there is no local tracking judge nearby. The certification track will be equivalent to a regular AKC track. A regulation track must be 440 to 500 yards long, with at least two right-angle turns out in the open. The track will be aged 30 minutes to 2 hours. The handler has two starting flags at the beginning of the track to indicate the direction started. The dog works on a harness and 40-foot lead and must work at least 20 feet in front of the handler. An article (either a dark glove or wallet) will be dropped at the end of the track, and the dog must indicate it but not necessarily retrieve it.

People always ask what the dog tracks. Initially, the beginner on the short-aged track tracks the tracklayer. Eventually, the dog learns to track the disturbed vegetation and learns to differentiate between tracks. Getting started with tracking requires reading the AKC regulations and a good book on tracking, in addition to finding other tracking enthusiasts. Work on the buddy system. That is, lay tracks for each other so you can practice blind tracks. It is possible to train on your own, but if you are a beginner, it is a lot more entertaining to track with a buddy. It's rewarding to see the dog use his natural ability.

Tracking Dog Excellent—TDX

The TDX track is 800 to 1,000 yards long and is aged three to five hours. There will be five to seven turns. An article is left at the starting flag, and three other articles must be indicated on the track. There is only one flag at the start, so it is a blind start. Approximately one and a half hours after the track is laid, two tracklayers will cross over the track at two different places to test the dog's ability to stay with the original track. There will be at least two obstacles on the track, such as a change of cover, fences, creeks, ditches, etc. The dog must have a TD before entering a TDX. There is no certification required for a TDX.

Variable Surface Tracking—VST

This test came into effect in September 1995. The dog must have a TD earned at least six months prior to entering this test. The track is 600 to 800 yards long and will have a minimum of three different surfaces. Vegetation will be included, along with two areas devoid of vegetation, such as concrete, asphalt, gravel, sand, hard pan, or mulch. The areas devoid of vegetation shall compose at least one-third to one-half of the track. The track is aged three to five hours. There will be four to eight turns and four numbered articles, including one leather, one plastic, one metal, and one fabric dropped on the track. There is one starting flag. The handler will work at least 10 feet from the dog.

Yorkshire Terriers are capable of participating in a variety of activities, including tracking and agility.

AGILITY

Agility was first introduced by John Varley at the Crufts Dog Show in England in February 1978, but Peter Meanwell, competitor and judge, actually developed the idea. It was officially recognized in the early 1980s. Agility is extremely popular in England and Canada and is growing in popularity in the US. The AKC acknowledged agility in August 1994. Dogs must be at least 12 months of age to be entered. It is a fascinating sport that the dog, handler, and spectators enjoy to the utmost.

Agility is a spectator sport in which the dog performs off lead. The handler either runs with his dog or positions himself on the course. He then directs his dog with verbal and hand signals over a timed course, over or through a variety of obstacles, including a time-out or pause. One of the main drawbacks to agility is finding a place to train. The obstacles take up a lot of space, and it is very time consuming to put up and take down courses.

The titles earned at AKC agility trials are Novice Agility Dog (NAD), Open Agility Dog (OAD), Agility Dog Excellent (ADX), and Master Agility Excellent (MAX). In order to acquire an agility title, a dog must earn a qualifying score in his respective class on three separate occasions under two different judges. The MAX will be awarded after earning ten qualifying scores in the Agility Excellent Class.

PERFORMANCE TESTS

During the last decade, the American Kennel Club has promoted performance tests—those events that test the different breeds' natural abilities. This type of event encourages a handler to devote even more time to his dog and retain the natural instincts of his breed heritage. It is an important part of the wonderful world of dogs.

Earthdog Events

Earthdog trials are for small terriers (Australian, Bedlington, Border, Cairn, Dandie Dinmont, Fox [Smooth and Wire], Lakeland, Norfolk, Norwich, Scottish, Sealyham, Skye, Welsh, and West Highland White) and Dachshunds.

Limited registration (ILP) dogs are eligible, and all entrants must be at least six months of age. The primary purpose of the small terriers and Dachshunds is to pursue quarry, to ground, hold the

Competing with your Yorkshire Terrier requires dedication and teamwork, but it is a rewarding experience.

game, alert the hunter where to dig, or to bolt. There are two parts to the test: (1) the approach to the quarry, and (2) working the quarry. The dog must pass both parts for a Junior Earthdog title (JE). The Senior Earthdog (SE) must do a third part—to leave the den on command. The Master Earthdog (ME) test is a bit more complicated.

(The above information has been taken from the AKC Guidelines for the appropriate events.)

GENERAL INFORMATION

Obedience, tracking, and agility allow the purebred dog with an Indefinite Listing Privilege (ILP) number or a limited registration to be exhibited and earn titles. Application must be made to the AKC for an ILP number.

The American Kennel Club publishes *Events*, a monthly magazine that is part of the *Gazette*, their official journal for the sport of purebred dogs. The *Events* section lists upcoming shows and the secretary or superintendent for them. The majority of the conformation shows in the US are overseen by licensed superintendents. Generally, the entry closing date is approximately two and a half weeks before the actual show. Point shows are fairly expensive, while the match shows cost about one-third of the point show entry fee. Match shows usually take entries the day of the show, but some are pre-entry. The best way to find match show information is through your local kennel club. Upon asking, the AKC can provide you with a list of superintendents, and you can write and ask to be put on their mailing lists.

Obedience trial and tracking test information is also available through the AKC. Frequently, these events are not superintended, but they are put on by the host club. Therefore, you should make the entry with the event's secretary.

There are numerous activities you can share with your dog. Regardless of what you do, it does take teamwork. Your dog can only benefit from your attention and training.

BEHAVIOR and Canine Communication

S tudies of the human/animal bond point out the importance of the unique relationships that exist between people and their pets. Those of us who share our lives with pets understand the special part they play through companionship, service, and protection. For many, the pet/owner bond goes beyond simple companionship; pets are often considered members of the family.

A leading pet food manufacturer recently conducted a nationwide survey of pet owners to gauge just how important pets were in their lives. Here's what they found:

- 76 percent allow their pets to sleep on their beds
- 78 percent think of their pets as their children
- 84 percent display photos of their pets, mostly in their homes
- 84 percent think that their pets react to their own emotions
- 100 percent talk to their pets
- 97 percent think that their pets understand what they're saying

Many people have unique relationships with their dogs and consider them to be members of the family.

Dogs teach children responsibility through the understanding of their care, feelings, and life cycles.

It has been proven that senior citizens show more concern for their own eating habits when given the responsibility of feeding a dog. Further, seeing that their dogs are routinely exercised encourages elderly owners to think of schedules that otherwise may seem unimportant to them. In addition, while the older owner may be arthritic and feeling poorly, having a dog may encourage him or her to become more active. Over the last few decades, pets have been shown to relieve the stress of those who lead busy lives, and owning a pet has even been known to lessen the occurrence of heart attack and stroke.

Many single people thrive on the companionship of their dogs. Lifestyles are very different than they used to be, and today more individuals seek the single life. However, they receive fulfillment from dog ownership. The majority of dogs, however, live in family environments. The companionship these pets provide is well worth the effort involved. Children in particular benefit from having a family dog. Dogs teach responsibility through the understanding of their care, feelings, and even respect for their life cycles. Frequently,

Today, an increasing number of dogs are working as service dogs trained to aid the blind and deaf.

those children who have not been exposed to dogs grow up afraid of them. Dogs can sense timidity, and some will take advantage of the situation.

Today, more dogs are working as service dogs, and many dogs are trained to aid the blind and deaf. Also, dogs are trained to provide multiple services for the disabled and are able to perform many different tasks for their owners. Search and rescue dogs, along with their handlers, are sent throughout the world to assist in the recovery of disaster victims. They are lifesavers. Some dogs become therapy dogs and are very popular with nursing homes and hospitals. The inhabitants of these establishments truly look forward to the dogs' visits.

Nationally, there is a Pet Awareness Week to educate students and others about the value and basic care of our pets. Many countries take an even greater interest in their pets than Americans do. In those countries, pets are allowed to accompany their owners into restaurants and shops. In the US, this freedom is only available to service dogs. Even so, people still think very highly of the human/animal bond.

Socialization and Training

Many prospective puppy buyers lack experience regarding the proper socialization and training needed to develop a desirable pet. In the first 18 months, training does take some work, but it is easier to start proper training before there is a problem that needs to be corrected.

The initial work begins with the breeder, who should start socializing the puppy at five to six weeks of age. Human socializing is critical up through 12 weeks of age and is likewise important during the following months. The litter should be left together during the first few weeks, but it is necessary to separate the pups by ten weeks of age. Leaving them together after that time will increase competition for litter dominance. If puppies are not socialized with people by 12 weeks of age, they will be timid later in life.

The eight- to ten-week age period can be a fearful time for puppies. They need to be handled very gently by children and adults. There should be no harsh discipline during this time. Starting at 14 weeks of age, the puppy begins the juvenile period, which ends when he reaches sexual maturity around 6 to 14 months

Your Yorkshire Terrier will benefit from socialization with all kinds of people, dogs, and other animals.

of age. During the juvenile period, he needs to be introduced to strangers (adults, children, and other dogs) on the home property. At sexual maturity, he will begin to bark at strangers and become more protective. A male will start to lift his leg to urinate, but you can inhibit this behavior by walking him on a leash away from trees, shrubs, fences, etc.

Puppy training classes are a great place to socialize your puppy with other dogs and start his training. However, make sure he has all his vaccinations before taking him to meet other dogs. Socialization and training are a crucial part of your dog's development and allow him to live as part of your household and family. In order for your dog to live harmoniously in your home, he should know the household rules. You should always be consistent; this way, your dog will know what is expected of him at all times. Even the most well-trained dogs may exhibit problem behaviors, often due to their natural instincts; for instance, some dogs are very vocal barkers, some dogs are born to dig, and some dogs will run and chase anything that moves. It takes consistent work and patience, but if your dog knows the rules, you can curb problem behaviors and help your dog to become part of the family.

Make sure your Yorkshire Terrier puppy has received all of his vaccinations before you allow him to play with other dogs.

PROBLEM BEHAVIORS

Barking

Barking can be a bad habit learned through the environment, and overzealous barking can be a breed tendency. When barking presents a problem for you, try to stop it as soon as it begins.

To solve barking problems, you first have to determine the cause. Perhaps the barking gets your attention—what your dog considers the perfect reward. If you run and bring him inside when he barks, he then learns that barking gets what he wants—you. He may also be barking because he's protecting your property from perceived (or real) threats, there may be other dogs or children playing nearby, he may be playing, or perhaps he's afraid of something. Again, like digging, some dogs are just more vocal than others and will always be barky, no matter what you do. However, you can control the noise factor through prevention and training.

The best way to stop outside "attention" barking is to ignore him until he realizes barking is futile and he quiets down. If it is bothering the neighbors, bring him inside and crate him, letting him out only when he's quiet.

In order for your Yorkshire Terrier to live harmoniously in your home, he must obey household rules.

Yelling at your dog may seem like the thing to do when he's barking, but it's actually counterproductive. To him, your yelling sounds like barking, and when you yell, he will bark more. Yelling just proves to him that the perceived threat is real, or else why would the pack leader be barking too?

If your dog is easily stimulated by what is going on outside, make sure you pull the curtains closed so that he isn't distracted by every leaf that blows by. Do not yell or make a fuss when he does bark. After he barks once or twice, tell him to be quiet and give him praise and a treat when he stops. Soon he will learn that he gets rewards for being quiet, not barking.

If your dog is barking inside the house when he is alone, he might be suffering from separation anxiety. A dog who has separation anxiety is inconsolable when you leave the house and will whine, bark, and perhaps scratch at the door. He may also destroy things while you're gone.

In order to help control this problem, don't make a big fuss about saying hello and goodbye when you enter or leave the house. In fact, don't greet your barking dog at all until he has calmed down. Ignore him. When you pet him, you're just rewarding the behavior. Only pet him when he has stopped barking and after you've asked him to sit.

Be sure to crate him or confine him to a safe room when you are gone so that he doesn't get a chance to destroy anything. Turn on the television or radio so that he feels like he has company. Make sure he gets plenty of exercise, and provide him with a chance to eliminate before you leave. Don't forget to give him plenty of chew toys to keep him occupied.

If your dog often barks his head off while in the crate, try this: About 30 minutes before you leave, give him his Nylabone® or a Rhino® stuffed with peanut butter or cheese and then ignore him just as if you were already gone. Don't talk to him, and don't say good-bye; just leave. (This also works if you don't leave your dog in a crate.) When you return, don't say hello or make a big deal about coming home; just walk right past the crate and ignore him for about five minutes. When he quiets down, take him directly outside to relieve himself. Don't take him out of the crate when he's barking. The rationale behind this is that if you acknowledge your dog the minute you get home, he'll anticipate your return and bark the entire time you're gone.

Another solution for barking due to separation anxiety is to pretend you're leaving as an exercise to get your dog used to your comings and goings. Place your dog in the crate, put on your coat, take your car keys, and walk around the house for a few minutes. Then, let him out if he's quiet and praise him. Next, dress up again and walk out the door for 30 seconds. Do it again for 2 minutes, then for 5 minutes, then for 10 minutes, then for 20 minutes, and so on. If he's quiet when you return, praise him verbally. If he's barking, just ignore him until he calms down, even if it's only for a moment. Repeat this exercise over a period of several days to several weeks, and your dog should get used to your leaving him.

Jumping Up

A dog who jumps up is a happy dog. Nevertheless, few guests appreciate dogs jumping on them.

Some trainers believe in allowing the puppy to jump up when he is a few weeks old. If you correct him too soon and at the wrong age, you may intimidate him and he could be timid around humans later in life. However, there will come a time, probably around four

Symptoms of separation anxiety include whining, barking, and scratching at the door when you leave the house.

months of age, when he needs to know when it is okay to jump and when he is to show good manners by sitting instead.

If you become irritated when your dog jumps up on you, then you should discourage it from the beginning. Jumping can actually cause harm or injury, especially to senior citizens or children. How, though, do you correct the problem? First, all family members need to participate in teaching the puppy to sit as soon as he starts to jump up. The sit must be practiced every time he does it. Don't forget to praise him for his good behavior. Let him know that he only gets petted if he sits first. If he gets up while being petted, stop petting him and tell him to sit again. Tell everyone in the household and anyone who visits not to touch your dog or give him any attention unless he earns it by sitting first.

If your dog is a really bad jumper, ask friends to help as well. Keep dog treats by the door and ask your visitors to tell your dog to sit when they come over. Keep him on his leash to help him remain under control, and have your guests give him the treat when he sits nicely. With time and patience, he will soon be sitting to greet everyone. Remember, the entire family must take part. Each time you allow your dog to jump up, you go back a step in training.

Running Away

There is little excuse for a dog to run away, because dogs should never be off leash except when supervised in a fenced-in yard.

Many prospective owners want to purchase a female because they believe a male is inclined to roam. It is true that an intact male is inclined to roam, which is one of the reasons a male should be neutered. However, females will roam also, especially if they are in heat. Regardless, these dogs should never be given this opportunity.

The first thing to remember is not to discipline your dog when you finally catch him after an escape. The reasoning behind this is that it is quite possible there could be a repeat performance, and you don't want your dog to be afraid to come to you when you call him.

Always kneel down when trying to catch a runaway. Dogs are afraid of people standing over them. Also, it would be helpful to have a treat or a favorite toy to help entice him to your side. After that initial runaway experience, start practicing the recall with your dog.

Puppies have to chew because their teeth and gums hurt while they are teething. When their adult teeth come in, they chew to clean and massage their teeth and gums.

Chewing

From 3 to 12 months of age, puppies chew on everything. In fact, they will chew shoes, newspapers, a neighbor's fingers—anything they can get their teeth on. Puppies don't chew out of spite or boredom; it's simply a natural behavior, relieving tension and anxiety. It's also just plain fun! In addition, puppies have to chew because their teeth and gums hurt while they are teething.

Stop your dog from chewing the wrong things by only allowing him to chew on his own toys. Never give him your old shoes, slippers, or socks—he won't be able to distinguish a new pair from an old one. Nylabone® products are great chew toys for both puppies and older dogs. Confining your dog to a crate whenever you can't keep an eye on him and puppy proofing your home will also help stop your dog from chewing on things he shouldn't. Remember, puppies *have* to chew. Even after their adult teeth come in, dogs chew to clean and massage their teeth and gums. Give them a safe alternative.

Biting, Nipping, and Mouthing

Biting, mouthing, and nipping are unacceptable behaviors, even in young dogs. What may seem cute in a little pup is not going to be so cute when he gets bigger.

Remember that rough play, wrestling, and tug-of-war aggravate and even teach these unwanted behaviors. Teasing your pup and playing chasing games can also encourage nipping. Your pup has an innate response to hunt and hold onto things. A simple game of tug-of-war means a lot more to your pup than it does to you.

When your puppy nips or bites you, snatch your hand away and say, "No! Ouch!" Then, stop playing with him and ignore him. If your puppy is really overexcited and won't calm down, put him in his crate. Your puppy must realize that you will only play with him and have fun with him if he plays nicely.

Also, be very careful when your puppy is playing with children. Kids can get just as overexcited as puppies do, and the games can get out of hand. Always supervise children and dogs when they are together, and if it gets too rough, institute a "time-out" and confine both the puppy and the child before someone gets hurt. Only let them play if they can be calm around each other.

Aggression

Any act of aggression on your puppy's part should be considered serious. Remember, your cute growling puppy may be an intimidating growling dog one day. If you socialize your puppy properly, you should not have an aggression problem. Remember, do not participate or allow rough play or wrestling, and don't praise your puppy for nipping.

Your puppy may become possessive regarding various things: his territory, his owners, or his food, or he might show aggression when he is scared. This is where training comes in handy. Your puppy must realize from the beginning that where he lives is *your* house and he is living by *your* rules. A pup who thinks he has to protect everything, including you, will be aggressive, and for good reason—he's got a big job. But if you teach him from the beginning that you are the leader, you shouldn't have a problem.

Your dog should let you take things away from him or approach his food bowl. He should not growl or snap. That bowl is *your* bowl, and that food is *your* food—you should be able to approach anytime you'd like. If you have this problem, approach the bowl with a treat; this will condition your dog to view you approaching the bowl as something pleasant. Keep doing it often, and always praise him when he gives things up. Then, make sure you give those things back to him as his reward for sharing.

Make sure that you supervise your dog when he is playing with children, because the play can get out of hand if both parties become overexcited.

Counter Surfing and Trash Spreading

Dogs jump up on tables because they are often rewarded with a tasty dinner, and the scents in your trash cans are just too hard to resist for most dogs. This behavior is best dealt with by preventing it in the first place. Don't give your dog human food, or if you're a softie, put the morsel in his dish and don't let him see that it has come from the counter or the table.

Good management will help to control this behavior. Avoid the counter problem by confining the dog and keeping him out of the kitchen or dining area when you can't supervise him. The simplest way to avoid a "trash hound" is to move the trash out of your dog's reach or buy a trash can with a cover that locks.

If your dog does get into the food he shouldn't, only correct him if you catch him in the act. Just like with housetraining, your dog won't associate the punishment with the food he stole an hour ago or the trash he knocked over this morning. Just chalk it up to experience and practice good management in the future.

Digging

Dogs dig because they're programmed to dig. Terriers, for example, "go to ground," meaning that they find prey in holes in the earth. To them, digging is fun and natural. Some dogs dig because they want to get out of a confined area, and others dig to release pent-up energy. They also dig to get away from the heat, so make sure your dog has plenty of drinking water and shady shelter when he's outside.

If you've got a particularly stubborn digger, you can fence off the places where you don't want him to dig and allocate a place in your yard where the dog will be allowed to dig. Let him know that it's okay for him to dig there by bringing him over to the spot and placing a toy or treat on the ground. Later, put it slightly under the dirt and maybe help him dig. When you catch him digging in the wrong place, bring him to his digging place. Show your approval by praising his digging in the right spot.

Stool Eating

Puppies do eat their own stool and even the stool of other animals. This is called coprophagia. It's not the most pleasant of things, but it's a normal habit, and most pups get over it as they grow older. The best solution is to keep your yard really clean and

If your Yorkie enjoys digging, fence off the areas you don't want him to dig and allocate a place where he can dig to his heart's content.

Ensuring that your Yorkshire Terrier is never off leash except when supervised in an enclosed, fenced-in yard will prevent him from running away.

take away the opportunity for your dog to eat anything he shouldn't. However, talk to your veterinarian, and after you have determined that it's not a medical condition or a health problem, ask him to prescribe a medicine that makes the waste taste terrible. You can also spray his waste with a bitter apple spray or vinegar—or both. If your pup gets into your cat's litter box, consider moving the box to another location. Sometimes changing a dog's diet and feeding him twice a day will stop coprophagia.

Submissive Urination

Some puppies urinate when they're particularly excited, like when you come home. Most pups who do this will grow out of the behavior in time. However, submissive dogs aren't urinating when the owner comes home because they are excited—they urinate because the leader has engaged them with some form of dominance, such as establishing eye contact, petting on the head and neck, or bending over them. The submissive wolf in the wild would immediately roll over and wet himself when challenged even slightly by a dominant member of the pack. Because you are the dominant member of your pack, the submissive wetter is just doing what seems natural.

The best way to treat this problem is by confining the dog to an area where he can't greet you or your guests right away—he has to get used to new stimuli gradually. Like with separation anxiety, make your comings and goings as low key as possible so the dog doesn't get overly excited.

Use treats instead of praise for successful greetings (no wetting). Manage the greeting of guests in a controlled area where wetting is okay (outside), and have the dog on a leash and in a sit so that he can't charge the guests in his excitement. Praise, praise, praise for each success, and have patience. The gentler you are to a dog who has this problem, the faster he will overcome it.

Carsickness

Carsickness usually starts during puppyhood, but if you train your puppy to enjoy riding in a car, you may avoid it. There are several causes of carsickness; the most common are the motion of the car, excitement, and anxiety.

Introduce your dog to the car gradually, while he's still young. Don't feed him just before or just after the ride. To accustom him

Over the last few decades, pets have been shown to relieve the stress of those who lead busy lives.

to the car, put him in it and praise him calmly, then take him out and praise him again, without going anywhere. Give him a treat if he'll take it. Follow this routine a few times until he begins to relax.

Now, put him back in the car and start the engine. After a minute, turn it off, take the puppy out, and play with him. Do this a few times, then take him for a short ride, perhaps halfway down the street. Again, play with him afterward. Do this training over an extended period of time when you're not in a rush.

When your dog becomes calm in the car, take him to the park or someplace that's fun for him. Remember that if he only rides in the car on the way to the veterinarian or to be dropped off at the boarding kennel, he might view the car as a negative experience.

Remember to make riding in the car an enjoyable experience. If possible, put him in a crate; he'll be more comfortable there than sitting between a couple of rowdy kids. There are even seat belts made for dogs. Make sure the car is not too hot, and never, ever leave your dog in the car with the windows closed, not even for two minutes. Besides being against the law, your dog could die of heatstroke.

Excessive Fear

Some dogs experience excessive fear directed toward a variety of events, like loud noises and other strange phenomena. The dog may beg to be held, or he may tremble in the corner or hide under the bed, looking around for any kind of comfort. While you may be tempted to coddle and soothe him, try to refrain from doing so. The problem with soothing a terrified dog is that it rewards his behavior— the exaggerated fear. He may learn that there is indeed something to be afraid of, and he'll remember that.

When dealing with excessive fear, it is best to ignore the dog when he's afraid for no good reason. If you must acknowledge his terror, just give him a little pat on the head, tell him it's going to be okay, and then go about your business. Give him a treat, or put the treats on the object he's afraid of if possible so that he associates it with positive things.

TRAVELING With Your Dog

The earlier you start traveling with your new puppy or dog, the better. He needs to become accustomed to traveling. When taking a trip, give consideration to what is best for your dog—traveling with you or boarding. When traveling by car, van, or motor home, you need to think ahead about locking your vehicle. In all probability, you have many valuables in the car and do not wish to leave it unlocked. Perhaps most valuable and not replaceable is your dog. Give a good deal of thought to securing your vehicle and providing adequate ventilation for your pet.

Other considerations when taking a trip with your dog are medical problems that may arise. Little inconveniences may also occur, such as exposure to external parasites. Some areas of the country are quite flea infested, so you may want to carry flea spray with you. This is even a good idea when staying in motels; quite possibly you are not the only occupants of the room.

Many motels and even hotels do allow canine guests, even some first-class establishments. There are many good books available that will tell you which hotels accept dogs and also help you plan a fun vacation with your canine companion. Call ahead to any motel or hotel that you may be considering and see if they accept pets. Sometimes it is necessary to pay a deposit against room damage. The management may feel reassured if you mention that your dog will be crated. If you do travel with your dog, take along plenty of plastic bags so that you can clean up after him. As a matter of fact, you should practice cleaning up everywhere you take your dog.

Depending on where you're traveling, you may need an up-to-date health certificate issued by your veterinarian. It is good policy to take along your dog's medical information, which would include the name, address, and phone number of your veterinarian, a vaccination record, rabies certificate, and any medication he is taking.

Car Rides

Some dogs are nervous riders and become carsick easily, so it is

When traveling to your destination by car, the safest place for your Yorkshire Terrier is in a crate.

helpful if your dog starts any trip with an empty stomach. If you continue taking him with you on short, fun rides, it will help accustom him to this experience more smoothly. Older dogs who tend to get carsick may have more of a problem adjusting to traveling. Those dogs who are having serious problems may benefit from medication prescribed by the veterinarian. Also, make sure to give your dog a chance to relieve himself before getting into the car. It is a good idea to be prepared for a cleanup with a leash, paper towels, bag, and terry cloth towel.

When in the car, the safest place for your dog is in a fiberglass or wire crate, such as the Nylabone® Fold-Away Pet carrier, although close confinement can promote carsickness in some dogs. An alternative to the crate is a car harness made for dogs and/or a safety strap attached to the harness or collar. Whatever you do, do not let your dog ride in the back of a pickup truck unless he is securely tied

Your Yorkshire Terrier's safety is very important, so supervise him closely when you travel to unfamiliar surroundings.

on a very short lead. If the vehicle stops abruptly, the dog could fall out and be dragged if the lead is too long.

Another advantage of the crate is that it is a safe place to leave your dog if you need to run into the store. Otherwise, you wouldn't be able to leave the windows down. However, in some states, it is against the law to leave a dog in the car unattended.

Never leave a dog loose in the car wearing a collar and leash. More than one dog has killed himself by hanging. Also, do not let him put his head out an open window. Foreign debris can be blown into his eyes. When leaving your dog unattended in a car, consider the temperature. It can take less than five minutes to reach temperatures over 100°F.

AIR TRAVEL

When traveling by air, you need to contact the airlines to check their policy regarding flying with your dog on board. Usually, you have to make arrangements up to a couple of weeks in advance when traveling with your dog. The airlines require your dog to travel in an airline-approved fiberglass crate. These can be purchased through the airlines, but they are also readily available in most pet-supply stores. The Nylabone® Fold-Away Pet Carrier is a perfect crate for air travel.

If your dog is not accustomed to a crate, it is a good idea to get him acclimated to it before your trip. The day of the actual trip you should withhold serving him water for about 1 hour ahead of departure and refrain from giving him food for about 12 hours. The airlines generally have temperature restrictions that do not allow pets to travel if it is either too cold or too hot. Frequently, these restrictions are based on the temperatures at the departure and arrival airports.

It's best to inquire about a health certificate. These usually need to be issued within ten days of departure. You should arrange for nonstop, direct flights, and if a commuter plane is involved, check to see if it will carry dogs. Some don't. The Humane Society of the United States has put together a tip sheet for airline traveling. You can receive a copy by sending a self-addressed, stamped envelope to:

The Humane Society of the United States
Tip Sheet
2100 L Street NW
Washington, DC 20037

A responsible, knowledgeable pet-sitter can care for your Yorkie if you and your family are unable to take him on vacation with you.

Regulations differ for traveling outside of the country and are sometimes changed without notice. You need to write or call the appropriate consulate or agricultural department for instructions well in advance of your trip. Some countries have lengthy quarantines (six months), and many differ in their rabies vaccination requirements. For instance, it may have to be given at least 30 days ahead of your departure.

Do make sure your dog is wearing proper identification, including your name, phone number, and city. You never know when you might be in an accident and separated from your dog, or your dog could be frightened and somehow manage to escape and run away.

Another suggestion would be to carry in-case-of-emergency instructions. These would include the address and phone number of a relative or friend, your veterinarian's name, address, and phone number, and your dog's medical information.

BOARDING KENNELS

Perhaps you have decided that you need to board your dog. Your veterinarian can recommend a good boarding facility or possibly a pet-sitter who will come to your house. It is customary for the boarding kennel to ask for proof of vaccination for the DHLPP, rabies, and bordetella vaccines. The bordetella should have been given within six months of boarding. This is for your protection. If the boarding kennel does not ask for this proof, you probably should not board at that kennel. Also, ask about flea control. Those dogs who suffer from fleabite allergy can get in trouble at a boarding kennel. Unfortunately, boarding kennels are limited as to how much they are able to do.

Some pet clinics have technicians who pet-sit and board clinic patients in their homes. This may be an alternative for you. Ask your veterinarian if he or she has an employee who can help you. There is a definite advantage to having a technician care for your dog, especially if he is a senior citizen or on medication.

IDENTIFICATION and Finding the Lost Dog

COLLARS AND TAGS

There are several ways of identifying your dog. The old standby is a collar with dog license, rabies tag, and ID tags. Unfortunately, collars have a way of being separated from dogs, and tags fall off, so it's important that they remain intact and on the dog. Collars and tags are the quickest form of identification.

TATTOOS

For several years, owners have been tattooing their dogs. Some tattoos use a number with a registry. Herein lies the problem, because there are several registries to check. If you wish to tattoo your dog, use your social security number. Humane shelters have the means to trace it.

Tattooing is usually done on the inside of the rear thigh. The area is first shaved and numbed. There is no pain, although some dogs do not like the buzzing sound. Occasionally, tattooing is not legible and needs to be redone.

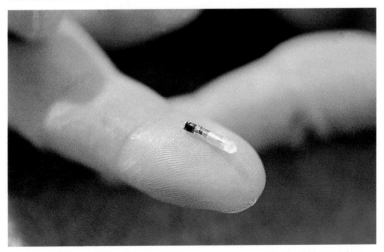

The microchip is a tiny device capable of identifying your dog should he ever become lost.

MICROCHIPS

The newest method of identification is microchipping. The microchip is a computer chip that is no larger than a grain of rice. The veterinarian implants it by injection between the shoulder blades. The dog feels no discomfort. If your dog is lost and picked up by the humane society, they can trace you by scanning the microchip, which has its own code. Most microchip scanners are friendly to other brands of microchips and their registries. The microchip comes with a dog tag saying that the dog is microchipped. It is the safest way of identifying your dog.

FINDING THE LOST DOG

Most people would agree that losing a dog is a tragedy. Responsible pet owners rarely lose their dogs because they keep them on a leash or in an enclosed yard. However, even dogs who are in fenced-in yards can get loose. Dogs find ways to escape either over or under fences. Another fast exit may be through the gate that perhaps someone left unlocked.

A fenced-in enclosure or yard is one way to keep your Yorkshire Terrier safe while outside.

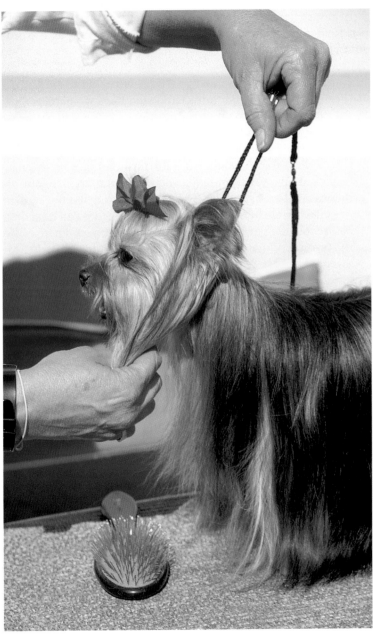

Your Yorkshire Terrier is less likely to become lost if you ensure that he always wears his collar and leash outside.

Below is a list that will hopefully be of help to you if you lose your pet. Remember, don't give up—keep looking. Your dog is worth your efforts.

1. Contact your neighbors and put flyers with a photo on them in their mailboxes. Include information like the dog's name, breed, sex, color, age, source of identification, when your dog was last seen and where, and your name and phone numbers. It may be helpful to say that the dog needs medical care. Offer a reward.
2. Check all local shelters daily. It is also possible that your dog may be picked up away from home and might end up in an out-of-the-way shelter. Check these, too. Go in person; it is not enough to call. Most shelters are limited on the time they can hold dogs before they are put up for adoption or euthanized. There is also the possibility that your dog will not make it to the shelter for several days. He could have been wandering or someone may have tried to keep him.
3. Notify all local veterinarians. Call and send flyers.
4. Call your breeder. Frequently, breeders are contacted when one of their dogs is found.
5. Contact the rescue group for your breed.
6. Contact local schools—children may have seen your dog.
7. Post flyers at schools, grocery stores, gas stations, convenience stores, veterinary clinics, groomers, and any other places that will allow them.
8. Advertise in the newspaper.
9. Advertise on the radio.

RESOURCES

BREED CLUB

Yorkshire Terrier Club of America, Inc. (YTCA)
Secretary: La Donna Reno
E-mail: ytca_sec@ytca.org
www.ytca.org

ORGANIZATIONS

American Kennel Club (AKC)
5580 Centerview Drive
Raleigh, NC 27606
Telephone: (919) 233-9767
Fax: (919) 233-3627
E-mail: info@akc.org
www.akc.org

Association of Pet Dog Trainers (APDT)
5096 Sand Road SE
Iowa City, IA 52240-8217
Telephone: (800) PET-DOGS
Fax: (856) 439-0525
E-mail: information@apdt.com
www.apdt.com

Canadian Kennel Club (CKC)
89 Skyway Avenue, Suite 100
Etobicoke, Ontario
M9W 6R4
Telephone: (416) 675-5511
Fax: (416) 675-6506
E-mail: information@ckc.ca
www.ckc.ca

Delta Society
580 Naches Avenue, SW Suite 101
Renton, WA 98055-2297
Telephone: (425) 226-7357
Fax: (425) 235-1076
E-mail: info@deltasociety.org
www.deltasociety.org

The Kennel Club
1 Clarges Street
London
W1J 8AB
Telephone: 0870 606 6750
Fax: 0207 518 1058
www.the-kennel-club.org.uk

United Kennel Club (UKC)
100 E. Kilgore Road
Kalamazoo, MI 49002-5584
Telephone: (269) 343-9020
Fax: (269) 343-7037
E-mail: pbickell@ukcdogs.com
www.ukcdogs.com

PUBLICATIONS

AKC Family Dog
American Kennel Club
260 Madison Avenue
New York, NY 10016
Telephone: (800) 490-5675
E-mail: familydog@akc.org
www.akc.org/pubs/familydog

Dogs Monthly
Ascot House
High Street, Ascot,
Berkshire SL5 7JG
United Kingdom
Telephone: 1344 628 269
Fax: 1344 622 771
E-mail: admin@rtc-associates.freeserve.co.uk
www.corsini.co.uk/dogsmonthly

ANIMAL WELFARE GROUPS AND RESCUE ORGANIZATIONS

American Society for the Prevention of Cruelty to Animals (ASPCA)
424 E. 92nd Street
New York, NY 10128-6804
Telephone: (212) 876-7700
www.aspca.org

Royal Society for the Prevention of Cruelty to Animals (RSPCA)
Telephone: 0870 3335 999
Fax: 0870 7530 284
www.rspca.org.uk

The Humane Society of the United States (HSUS)
2100 L Street, NW
Washington DC 20037
Telephone: (202) 452-1100
www.hsus.org

VETERINARY RESOURCES

American Veterinary Medical Association (AVMA)
1931 North Meacham Road-Suite 100
Schaumburg, IL 60173
Telephone: (847) 925-8070
Fax: (847) 925-1329
E-mail: avmainfo@avma.org
www.avma.org

British Veterinary Association (BVA)
7 Mansfield Street
London
W1G 9NQ
Telephone: 020 76366541
Fax: 020 74362970
E-mail: bvahq@bva.co.uk
www.bva.co.uk

INDEX

Adoption, 51-54, 156
Aggression, 36, 38, 96, 140
Agility, 43, 108, 120, 126, 128
Air travel, 150
America, 11, 14
American Kennel Club (AKC), 10, 12, 14, 18, 19, 20, 39, 43, 46, 70, 107, 111, 113, 114, 118, 120, 122, 124, 126, 128
Anal sac impaction/ inflammation, 91
Anesthesia, 54, 74, 76
Animal shelter, 43
Anxiety, 139, 144
Arthritis, 45, 76, 130
Barking, 34, 133, 134-137
Bathing, 60-64, 68, 91
Behavior, 129-146
Belgium, 18
Biting, 38, 71, 139-140
Bleeding, 77
Boarding kennel, 85, 146, 152
Booster vaccinations, 80
Bordetella (kennel cough), 83
Bordetella vaccine, 80, 152
Breed club, 39, 52
Breeder(s), 11, 16, 39, 40, 43, 51, 52, 54, 58, 59, 77, 79, 91, 95, 113, 118, 132, 156,
—finding, 39-43
Breeding, 11, 16, 40, 43, 98-106
Broken-Haired Scotch Terrier, 10
Brushing, 59-60, 62, 63, 68, 70
Burns, 55, 77
Canada, 14, 114, 126
Canadian Kennel Club, 107
Canine Good Citizen® Certificate, 112
Canine Good Citizen® Program, 108, 111-112

Caring, 55-70
Car rides, 147-150
Carsickness, 144, 147, 148
Characteristics, 34-38
Chewing, 55, 71, 72, 76, 86, 92, 100, 139
Chew toy(s), 72, 74, 136, 139
Cheyletiella, 90-91
Children, 38, 56, 130, 133, 134, 140, 156
Clydesdale Terrier, 9
Coat, 9, 19, 20, 34, 38, 48-50, 52, 59, 60, 62, 63, 64, 65, 67, 68, 69, 70, 77
Coccidiosis, 86
Colitis, 91
Collar, 89, 150, 153
Conformation, 43, 95, 108, 112-122
Conjunctivitis, 91-92
Coronavirus, 85
Coronavirus vaccine, 80
Counter surfing, 141
Crackering, 68-69
Crate, 55, 68, 121, 134, 136, 137, 139, 140, 146, 147, 148, 150
Crufts, 119-120
Demodectic mange, 90
Dental care, 71-76
DHLPP, 79, 80, 152
Diarrhea, 77, 82, 83, 85, 86
Diet, 58, 77, 91, 92
Diet sheet, 106
Digging, 133, 134, 142
Disease, 82-85, 92
Distemper, 79, 82
Dog show, 10, 39, 108, 112, 118, 119
Down, 110, 112, 122, 123
Down-stay, 110
Ear care, 64
Ear infection, 92
Ear mites, 64
Earthdog, 126-128
England, 8, 9, 10, 11, 12, 14, 107, 116, 118, 119, 126

English Terrier, 8
Events, 128
Excessive fear, 146
Exercise, 56, 97
External parasites, 88-91, 147
Family, 129, 130, 133, 138
Feeding, 43, 52, 77, 100, 101, 104, 144
Feeding and Nutrition, 58-59
Field trials, 10, 108
Flea(s), 86, 92, 94, 147, 152
Fleabite allergy, 92-94, 152
Flea collars, 88
Food, 39, 58, 71, 72, 92, 94, 97, 101, 104, 140, 141
Fun matches, 113, 123
Gazette, 128
Giardiasis, 86
Great Britain, 20, 113
Grooming, 39, 51, 59-70, 94, 121
—bathing, 60-64, 68, 91
—brushing, 59-60, 62, 63, 68, 70
—ear care, 64
—for show, 70
—nail care, 70
—pet trims, 64-68
Hair, 38, 46, 48, 60, 62, 63, 64, 65, 67, 68, 69, 91, 92
Handling, 56
Harness, 124, 148
Health care, 77-97
Health certificate, 147, 150
Heartworm, 80, 88
Heel, 110, 122, 123
Hepatitis, 79, 82
History, 8-18
Hookworms, 85-86
Household dangers, 55-56
Housetraining, 52, 56-58, 96, 141
Huddersfield Ben, 10

Humane shelters, 79, 153
Humane Society of the
    United States, 150
Hunter, 34
Hypoglycemia, 58
Immunizations, 79, 80
Indefinite Listing Privilege
    (ILP), 126, 128
Industrial Revolution, 9
Interdigital cysts, 94
Internal parasites, 86-88
Intestinal parasites, 79, 80,
    85-86
Jumping up, 137-138
Junior showmanship, 120,
    122
Kennel Club, 10, 20, 46,
    70, 107, 116, 119
Kennels, 14
Lameness, 94
Leash, 108, 110, 112, 138,
    144, 148, 150, 154
Leptospirosis, 79, 82
Leptospirosis vaccine, 56
Lyme, Connecticut, 85
Lyme disease, 80, 85, 89
Manchester Terrier, 8
Match shows, 128
Microchips, 154
Nail care, 64
Neutering, 46, 54, 106
Non-Sporting Group, 10
Nylabone®, 55, 72, 74,
    136, 139
Nylabone® Fold-Away Pet
    Carrier, 148, 150
Obedience, 108, 111, 120,
    121, 122-124, 128
Obedience Regulations, 124
Oiling, 68
Paisley Terrier, 9
Parainfluenza, 79
Parasites, 72, 79, 80, 85-91,
    147
—external, 88-91, 147
—internal, 86-88
—intestinal, 79, 80, 85-86
Parvovirus, 79, 82-83
Parvovirus vaccine, 79

Pedigree, 10, 11, 43
Periodontal disease, 74-76
Personality, 19, 39, 50, 51
Pet Awareness Week, 132
Pet trims, 64-68
Physical exams, 77-79
Poor skin, 94
Praise, 58, 108, 111, 136,
    138, 140, 144, 146
Pregnancy, 101
Problem behaviors, 134-
    146
Puppy kindergarten, 108,
    110, 113
Rabies, 83
Rabies certificate, 147
Rabies vaccine, 80, 152
Recall, 110-111, 122, 138
Registration, 43, 52, 106,
    107, 126
Reward(s), 134, 136, 140,
    146, 156
Rhino®, 136
Rocky Mountain Spotted
    Fever, 89
Roundworms, 86
Running away, 138
Sarcoptic mange, 90
Scotland, 9
Seizures, 77
Selecting, 39-54
Separation anxiety, 136,
    137, 144
Shelters, 156
Sit, 108-110, 111, 112,
    122, 123, 136, 138, 144
Sit-stay, 110
Socialization, 51, 56, 140
Socialization and training,
    132-133
Spaying, 54, 95-97
Sport, 107-128
Sporting Group, 10
Standard, 19-33, 43, 112,
    113
—American Kennel Club
    breed standard, 25-27
—interpretation of the
    standards, 27-33

—Kennel Club breed
    standard, 20-24
Stay, 110, 112
Stool eating, 142-144
Submissive urination, 144
Tapeworms, 86-88
Tattoos, 153
Teeth, 46, 71, 72, 76, 139
Temperament, 19, 50-51,
    95
Ticks, 89
Tonsillitis, 94
Topknot, 60, 68, 69, 70
Toy(s), 138, 139, 142
Tracking, 43, 108, 124-
    125, 128
Trainers, 137
Training, 36, 108, 110,
    113, 123, 128, 132, 133,
    134, 138, 146
Trash spreading, 141
Traveling, 147-152
Treat(s), 74, 108, 111, 136,
    138, 140, 142, 144, 146
United States, 10, 116, 118,
    119, 126, 128, 132
Vaccination(s), 43, 52, 56,
    72, 77, 79, 80, 82, 83,
    85, 104, 106, 112, 133
Vaccination record, 147
Vaccination sheet, 106
Veterinarian, 43, 45, 46,
    52, 54, 56, 59, 64, 72,
    74, 76, 77, 79, 82, 85,
    88, 91, 92, 94, 96, 100,
    102, 103, 106, 144, 146,
    147, 148, 152, 154, 156
Vomiting, 77, 82, 83, 85, 86
Watchdog, 34-36
Waterside Terrier, 8
Westie trim, 65-67
Westminster, 12, 15, 118-
    119
Whipworms, 86
World War I, 11
Wrapping, 68-69
Yorkshire Terrier Club of
    America, 12, 14, 39, 103
Yorkshire, England, 8, 9